YOUR CUSTOMER IS THE STAR

YOUR CUSTOMER IS THE STAR

How to Make Millennials, Boomers and Everyone Else
Love Your Business

Micah Solomon

Printed in the United States of America
First Printing, MMXV
Library of Congress Cataloging-in-Publication Data

Your Customer Is the Star: How To Make Millennials, Boomers, and Everyone Else Love Your Business, written by Micah Solomon

Front cover design: Dan Schuman
Art Direction: Jorge Krüger

We offer significant discounts for bulk purchases of 50 or more.

ISBN: 151172997X
ISBN 13: 9781511729970

Contents

Introduction

There's an assumption long held in business that's only halfway true: that customer service is a fundamental, timeless concept whose unchanging principles hearken back to classical Greek and Biblical models, with bad service clearly distinguishable from good service and inhospitality the simple opposite of hospitality. This tidy formulation misses that *the particulars* of how service has been delivered within our own lifetimes—a returns counter, a cash register, a line where the customer waits to reach the register for the privilege of paying and leaving—are artifacts of recent history that may no longer reflect the reality of how today's customers want to be served.

Your Customers—All of Them—Have Changed

Customers today of all ages think differently about customer service and the customer experience. Consumers today are buying (or deciding not to), raving about your customer service (or telling their friends to avoid you), enhancing (or depressing) your bottom line based on factors your business may have never considered.

It's important to get a fix on this, and quickly, because the changes that customers have already begun to clamor for are just a whisper compared to what's about to come. Every trend that affects your business subtly today will actively confront your company within a few years, as younger customers enter the marketplace and revolt against the archaic ways you're still doing business.

Changes on Steroids: The Arrival of the Millennial Generation

One reason this message is so urgent is demographic. Within the next few years, millennial customers–born between 1980 and 2000 (give or take)–will bring to your business the greatest spending power of any generation to date. They'll be spending on this unparalleled scale because their sheer numbers are unprecedented: This generation is even larger than the baby boom at its height. And if you don't adapt, you'll miss out on this generational windfall.

Millennials' expectations as customers have been shaped by the generation's lifetime immersion in the fast-evolving worlds of online commerce, search engines and on-the-go connectivity. The phones these young people use have always been smart. The Internet has always been on. These are customers who've likely never waited in line at the bank, who've rarely waited for letters to arrive by mail, who've seldom had their musical choices limited to the radio or what can fit on a mass-marketed CD. Millennials have grown up at a time when it's possible to align their shopping with their values—the chance to choose humane, green, fair trade, organic, employee owned and so forth, or not.

I will spend a good amount of time in this book talking about millennials because of their sheer numbers and direct economic importance, and because their preferences and behaviors are increasingly bleeding into the customer behavior of older generations. In other words, if you're in business today, it makes good economic sense to focus on millennial customer expectations because millennials' purchasing power is so valuable (and growing), and also because their digitally driven expectations are spreading so quickly to other generations. The standard expectation of a 25-year-old customer today will be mirrored in the expectations of her mom and dad as well in a very short time.

The Opportunity and the Challenge

Serving customers today, and tomorrow, means finding the best ways to streamline the customer experience via technology, and it means delivering the warmest, most genuine human-to-human customer service where such service makes a difference. This isn't easy. Adapting our mindset to successfully serving new and rapidly evolving customers will take your attention, creativity and hard work. Don't make the mistake of missing this opportunity.

1

Meet the Most Important Generation of Customers in History: The Millennials

Here's the story you already know. Millions of soldiers, sailors and airmen return from World War II to the embrace of millions of Rosie the Riveters, apparently *very* riveting Rosies, judging by the fruitful output of these couples during the postwar decades: 2.4 children per couple, the biggest generation America has ever seen. These kids, the Baby Boomers, grow up to transform the social and economic landscape of a nation.

Now, here's the story you've heard less often, if ever: The baby boom has happened again, and then some. The Boomers themselves, in the fullness of time, have given birth to an even bigger generation. Their offspring, the millennials (also known as Gen Y), are the young adults and teenagers born between 1980 and 2000 who are poised to transform a nation once more.

The Biggest Generation of Customers Ever

The millennial generation is already more numerous than any other generation, even that of the Baby Boomers, and will only, comparatively speaking, grow larger as the populations of older generations dwindle, both in the U.S. (this book's primary focus) and worldwide.

Now, the snarky headlines you've seen regarding this new generation may have you thinking, "Who gives a shade-grown shiitake about pleasing and retaining millennial customers? Aren't they ramen-eating, impecunious and underemployed?" Well, not exactly—and certainly not for long. With a wallet power that's growing quickly and will soon exceed that of the Boomers, millennials are about to become a very big deal for most brands. It's estimated they'll be spending $200 billion annually by 2017 and $10 trillion over their lifetimes as consumers.

Defining the Generations

Allow me a minute to define the generations of customers we encounter today. I'll keep this quick and approximate as I'm a businessman, not an academic.

- *Silent Generation:* Born between 1925 and 1940, give or take a few years, this is the generation defined by the Great Depression and world war they experienced as kids and young adults.
- *Baby Boomers:* The postwar cohort of customers that has dominated social discourse and economic activity for the last several decades. According to the Census Bureau, this generation was born between 1946 and 1964. Sometimes, the baby boom is divided by demographers into the earlier baby boom, born 1946 to 1953, and the later Generation Jones, born 1954 to 1965.
- *Gen X:* Born in the early or mid-1960s through 1980, this generation is almost a blip, demographically speaking, especially if you remove the years (the early 1960s) from this generation that overlap the more traditional definition of the baby boom.
- *Millennials (or Gen Y):* The generation born approximately between 1980 and 2000 that will be the focus of this chapter.

Put Your Money Where the Math Is

The millennial generation is not only the biggest generation in history, it's still growing (in the U.S.) thanks to immigration. Meanwhile, advancing age and decrepitude are bringing Boomers—as it has already brought the Silent Generation before them—to the cusp of a slow fade as consumers.

Millennials will soon become by far the most important consumers encountered by businesses, both in number of interactions and dollars spent. In business travel (an excellent proxy for a wide range of spending activity), the millennial generation will account for nearly 50% of all business flights by 2020, according to Boston Consulting Group. In other words, they'll equal the spending of *all* other generations combined not terribly long after you read this. In contrast, by 2020 Boomers will account for just 16% of business flights, dwindling to 11% by 2025, according to the BCG estimate.

To be fair, there have been claims to the contrary regarding this looming drop-off in Boomer spending. The *New York Times* has run not one but two pieces on the failure of Boomer spending to fade as quickly as predicted, but whatever truth there is to this rebuttal, it's a temporary one. There's no way around the biological reality: As body parts get creaky or give way entirely, spending gets harder to do. In addition, it becomes more appealing to base your spending on your kids' wishes and advice: kids who, in the case of Boomers, are millennials.

The most ambitious rebuttal comes from Boomer scientist Dr. Ray Kurzweil, who has plotted out—proven, he would say—exactly how medical advances will let the good doctor and his cogenerationists live forever. Dr. Kurzweil—kid you I do not—means this literally. Kurzweil's expectations aside, Boston Consulting Group estimates that by 2030 there will only be 56 million Boomers alive compared to 78 million hale-and-hearty millennials, smoke-free (for the most part) and wearing their seat belts or bicycle helmets.

To begin to understand what millennials expect when they shop, let's look at some generational characteristics. I'll concentrate on those characteristics likely to have business relevance as the millennials rise to prominence as consumers.

1. Millennials Accept Technology as a Given—and as Part of Their Identity.

They've grown up with digital devices that bundle communication, entertainment, shopping, mapping and education all in one. From an early age, smartphone use has been the norm. Millennials have always had Internet at home and in school. MP3 players have long offered them ubiquitous music options. Even their first political memories revolve around technology, from navigating the innovative Barack Obama campaign website (well, innovative for politics) to supporting activist campaigns on Facebook. Compare this to more traditional defining moments in early politicization: volunteering at a phone bank, stuffing mailers, standing outside in the rain 'til the polls finally close.

Naturally, then, millennials embrace and align themselves with technology. Because of this identification with technology, millennials tend to adopt new technology more quickly compared with the more skeptical approach of previous generations.

... Which Means they Expect Technology to Always Work, and to Work Easily

Technology has become far more user friendly during millennials' lifetimes, particularly when compared to what previous generations encountered. The relentless focus on simplifying the user interface at Apple, Amazon, Google and lesser-known technology players has set a new standard of intuitiveness across the tech industry that millennials accept as the norm. Businesses should be careful not to throw clunky, alienating devices or websites at these customers and expect patience or understanding as customers struggle to find a workaround.

At San Francisco-based Zendesk, a SaaS (software as a service) company that both sells to and employs millennials, Gen Xer Pam Dodrill (who has since moved on to ServiceMax) made this point colorfully to me. "Millennials are more tech-dependent than we were, which is what drives their expectation that there should be fewer problems. Think about it: We rode our bikes, and we jumped in the creek. *That* was the technology our generation depended on. Imagine what would have happened if our bikes kept breaking or our sneakers kept needing to be rebooted."

Dodrill's then-colleague at Zendesk, J.D. Peterson (now at Scriptd), added: "Millennials simply expect technology to work, because that's been their experience. Remember the 'blue screen of death' that users would get on their PCs? And how Mac users had the dreaded icon of a bomb when things went bad? When I've made these references to millennials, they don't even register, because the computers and devices they've grown up with essentially never crash."

… And Mobile Is the Technology Closest to Their Hearts.
Millennials (in large part) don't watch TV, don't go to church and don't, it appears, dream—they text. According to Pew, more than four out of five sleep with or next to their cell phones. They own more cell phones, use their cell phones more, text more and text while driving (yikes) more than other generations. They're also more likely to own a cell phone as their only phone: 41% have no landline.

Of course, millennials don't use smartphones just for texting. More than twice as many millennials as non-millennials use a mobile device to research products and read user reviews while shopping, according to marketer Jeff Fromm, whose company, Barkley, has researched the subject. Millennials even donate to charities and causes through their mobile devices. In fact, among those who donate, nearly 50% do it by phone.

Smartphones, in other words, are the new catchall: a concierge, a style advisor, a bar for hookups and so on. In this generation that rarely smokes, cell phones have even replaced smoking as the thing to do in those lonely moments when existential angst threatens to encroach.

2. They're a Social Generation—In Almost Everything They Do.

Millennials are a sociable generation. And for millennials, this sociability is expressed online as well as in real life ("IRL"), particularly in the arenas where online and offline activities and circles of friends overlap. Offline, millennials are more likely than other generations to shop, dine and travel with groups, whether these are organized interest groups, less formal groupings of peers or excursions with extended family, according to Boston Consulting Group data. Online, their sharing habits on Facebook, Snapchat and other social sites, and the opinions they offer on Yelp, TripAdvisor and Amazon, reflect their eagerness for connection, as do their electronic alerts to friends and followers (via Foursquare et al.) that show off where they are, where they're coming from and where they're headed—online alerts that reflect and affect behavior in the physical world.

This social behavior has big implications for those of us who serve customers. "A shopping habit that sets millennials apart from non-millennials is their tendency to shop in groups and seek the opinions of others," says marketer Jeff Fromm. More than two-thirds of millennials, according to Fromm's research, "don't make a major decision until they have discussed it with a few people they trust," compared to around half of all non-millennials. Seventy percent of millennials are "more excited about a decision they've made when their friends agree with them, compared to 48% of non-millennials," Fromm continues. Female millennials in particular regard shopping as a group activity, shopping twice as often with their spouses, friends or family members as do non-millennial women.

Millennials don't consume food, beverages, services, products or media in silence. They eat noisily (so to speak) and very visually. They review, blog and Tumblr, update Wikipedia entries and post Youtube, Vine and

Instagram videos. Often these posts concern their consumption activities, interests and aspirations. All told, as Boston Consulting Group reports, "the vast majority of millennials report taking action on behalf of brands and sharing brand preferences in their social groups."

We're not cyborgs yet but in many ways, with the tools at millennials' fingertips in particular, it can feel like we're getting close. McCann Worldwide conducted a study ("The Truth About Youth") in 2011 of 7,000 youngsters that turned up this curious finding: 48% of 23- to 30-year-olds would be willing to give up their sense of smell in return for being able to keep their laptop or phone. (With great restraint, McCann avoided calling this question "the sniff test," but I lack such self-control.)

Here's another revolutionary fact about millennials: They get along with their parents. According to Pew, teenagers today get into fewer fights with their parents than Mom and Dad did with theirs as teens. According to Joeri Van den Bergh and Mattias Behrer, authors of *How Cool Brands Stay Hot,* an insightful book about marketing and the millennial generation, six out of 10 teens eat with their family four or more nights per week. Incredibly, 85% of teens name one of their parents as their best friend, rather than naming a peer. And more than a third of millennials of all ages say they influence what products their parents buy, what shops and restaurants they visit and what trips they take.

This striking lack of conflict between generations means that millennials can be vital carriers of a business's commercial message to not only their friends but also their parents. At the rate they're spreading the word, it won't be long until almost everyone passes for a millennial, as far as attitude and buying patterns go.

3. They Collaborate and Cooperate.
Among millennials there's less substance abuse, crime and teen pregnancy compared to earlier generations (at the same age), as well as higher

community participation rates and academic test scores, according to research by Morley Winograd and Michael D. Hais, all of which points to the seriousness and collaborative nature—what I call a "we can fix it together" mentality—of this generation.

Millennials want everyone to get along, and they think everyone should be able to. As Van den Bergh and Behrer put it, "Contrary to previous generations, Gen Yers were brought up in an atmosphere of equal relationships and co-decision-making," what Winograd and Hais describe as an upbringing focused on collaborating between the generations based on mutually determined goals. Parents and educators throughout their childhood emphasized collaboration and cooperation, and so did the shows they grew up with: Millennials cut their TV teeth on the educational television shows *Bob the Builder, Blue's Clues* and *Barney and Friends.* In the award-winning *Blue's Clues,* all the characters cooperate, compromise and collaborate to solve the educational puzzle of the day. On *Barney and Friends*, there's no conflict to be found anywhere. Each week on the animated *Bob the Builder,* the show's lead character (that would be "Bob") responds to a problem that has arisen in that episode with the question, "Can we fix it?" to which the supporting characters respond in unison, "Yes we can!" (My daughter, born at the tail end of the millennial period, changed her name in nursery school to "Bob" in homage to the cartoon and would use the following technique to win a family decision on where to eat: "I think we should all cooperate and go where I want to go—to McDonald's!")

Millennials enjoy the possibility of collaborating with businesses and brands, as long as they believe their say matters to the company in question. They don't necessarily see a clear boundary between the customer and the brand, the customer and marketer, or the customer and service provider. Alex Castellarnau at Dropbox, the popular file transfer service, put it to me this way: With millennials, "a new brand, service or product is only *started* by the company; it's finished by the customers. Millennials are a generation that wants to co-create the product, the brand, with you. Companies that understand this and figure out ways to engage in this co-creation relationship with millennials will have an edge."

4. They're Looking for Adventure (and Whatever Comes Their Way). Millennial customers crave the joy of adventures and discoveries, whether epic or everyday. Millennials often view commerce and even obligatory business travel as opportunities rather than burdens, due to the adventures that can be had along the way. I'm reluctant to chalk up this phenomenon to youthful wanderlust alone, because the breadth of experiences this generation craves suggests there's something more at work:

- When shopping, they prefer what's known as an "experiential lifestyle environment" (a retail environment where shopping is not just a transaction and the pleasure of being in the store isn't limited to the goods customers take home). [1]
- Far more millennials than non-millennials report a desire to visit every continent and travel abroad as much as possible.[2]
- More than twice as many millennials as those in other age brackets say they are willing "to encounter danger in pursuit of excitement."[3] This may sound irrelevant to you as a businessperson if you don't sell bungee ropes or the like, but consider the idea of "danger" more broadly than actual risk to life or limb. Embracing danger as a customer can mean traveling across the city for artisanal cupcakes, knowing that there's a high risk of disappointment since the bakery famously sells out each day before 10 a.m., or shopping, as a lark, at a popup store with no history and nothing but word of mouth to recommend it.
- When millennials dine out, for example, they're often in search of something exotic, adventuresome, memorable or new to explore

during their dining experience. This has helped transform cuisine searches ("tastespotting") into an adventure—and food-truck-following (a concept sure to evoke fears of stomachache in some of their elders) into its own culture. [4]

5. They're Passionate About Values.

Millennials are a highly values-driven generation, specifically in terms of the attributes that Winograd and Hais call "civic" values: the virtues that relate to good citizenship.[5] This can be attributed to their upbringing, say Winograd and Hais in *Millennial Momentum,* a volume that focuses on the politics of this generation. While growing up, "young millennials were revered, praised, sheltered, befriended and carefully guided by their parents to lead well-structured lives based on adherence to clear and mutually agreed-upon rules. This has produced a generation of young people that is, by most measures, accomplished, self-confident, group-oriented and optimistic." Boomer parents have taught their children that every voice matters, that bullying is bad and equality is worth fighting for, that it takes a village. In large part, this generation polls as a gentle, loving generation; specifically speaking, polls conducted at a similar age with previous generations display far fewer of these civic-values inclinations.[6]

More millennials than non-millennials integrate their beliefs and causes into their choice of companies to support, their purchases and their day-to-day interactions. More than 50% of millennials make an effort to buy products from companies that support the causes they care about, according to research from Barkley, an independent advertising agency. They're twice as likely to care about whether or not their food is organic than are their nonmillennial counterparts. When you consider how money-strapped many millennials remain, their willingness to put a premium on such issues is striking. [7]

Millennials are concerned with more than political and ethical issues. They also care about what's genuine and authentic. This interest falls some-where between a purely aesthetic preference and a search for honesty, for truth. And it's a powerful force for motivating millennial customers.

A Warning About Generalizations, Including Mine

I've provided a number of generalizations here in this chapter that I find valuable in understanding and, ultimately, successfully serving millennials as customers. But I want to add a caveat to these generational generalizations.

Your customer is an individual first and a millennial (or a Baby Boomer or a member of the Silent Generation) second. Knowledge of a macro trend can make you a lot of money over time. However, it's something that can also cost you dearly if your eyes are on the proverbial forest and you stop seeing, and serving, the individual trees. Even if my descriptions, on average, suit your customer's generational cohort to a T, the specific customer in front of you may not.

Also note that what a specific customer has in common with her generation may be less important than what is happening to her right now: She's in a hurry, or she's feeling leisurely. Her dog just died. Her rabbit just gave birth to octuplets. She just got out of a long-term relationship. Or she doesn't like your receptionist's cologne. Think about it this way: You come across a Facebook group called "Millennial Moms." While the millennial part would certainly make up a part of its members' identity, the "Moms" part, it's pretty safe to guess, would be a big chunk of that identity well.

Conversely, don't assume these generalizations apply only to millennials. Because of millennials' influence on their elders, as well as their elders' increasing comfort level with technology, many expectations and behaviors that are now standard for millennials will soon spread to the majority of customers.

As Christopher Hunsberger, EVP Global Products and Innovation, Four Seasons Hotels and Resorts, tells me, "Millennials are an important group of guests in their own right. But their significance is more than that: They're a unique group in terms of their impact on the rest of our customer base. The behaviors and expectations of the millennial group of guests tend to shape the thinking of the rest of us."

To use jargon (something I try to avoid doing), what Hunsberger is saying here is that the psychographics—"the study and classification of people according to their attitudes, aspirations and other psychological criteria"— of millennials are becoming more and more applicable to older generations. If you truly understand the psychographics of millennial customers, this knowledge will ultimately trump demographics—and your resulting decision-making could bring you success across many generations.

2

The (Unauthorized) Jetsons Guide to Modern Customer Service

Building the right experience for today's customers requires you to think hard about an uncomfortable subject: where human employees are helpful to customers, and where they just get in the way.

Today's customers often *do* want you out of the way. Millennials, and those who share a millennial outlook, hold different ideas about where human-powered service fits into the customer experience. Younger customers, through years of experience with online and self-service solutions, have grown used to the way technology can reduce the need for human gatekeepers to ensure accuracy and manage data. So the last thing they want is for your employees to gum up the works without adding value.

Think for a moment about how many transactions customers today routinely conduct without any human interaction. They make dinner reservations, sign up for classes, review schoolwork and grades, schedule and reschedule medical appointments. Previously, all of these transactions required contact with another human. Now, thanks to technological advances, they can often be carried out without uttering a word to a single employee. All of us who travel by air have grown accustomed to airlines' use of technology to put the passenger in the driver's seat (if you'll allow me to gleefully mangle a metaphor). A passenger making a flight reservation can scroll through and select the class of service, departure time, even the specific seat on the plane. Then, she enters her own hard-to-spell last name and any special services required, prints a boarding pass or sends it to her mobile device from home at 2 a.m., and soundly falls asleep. In handling such transactions without the intervention of employees, customers have discovered that technology often takes care of such logistical functions faster and more capably than when employees insert themselves into the equation.

The (Unauthorized) Jetsons Test

I have a colorful little test you can use to determine the service functions that belong on either side of the human/technology divide—that is, which services you should offload to technology and which ones you should keep in the hands of your employees. I call it my Jetsons Test, based on the 1962 television series set 100 years in the future.

Here's what customer service looks like in the Jetsons' vision of the future.

Much of the customer service is provided by machines. And much of this machine-based service is actually self-service: ordering breakfast from an automated menu at home, using a dictating machine that records onto rewriteable LP records. (Don't snicker—they got this prediction at least 75% right.)

The service provided by humans adds what people want out of human interaction: warmth and a little drama. Consider the friendly southern-accented receptionist who provides a warm greeting at the factory where George Jetson works, or consider Henry, the apartment building's superintendent who does a bit of handiwork here and there but whose primary function is to be buddies with the Jetson family.

This is a solid model for dividing your operations. If someone can do the job more efficiently or effectively than a machine, then a human should be doing it (cardiac surgery and watercolor painting both fall in this category). And if a person can do the job more *warmly* than a machine, assign that task as well to the warm-blooded. Otherwise, leave it to the machines.

The exceptions are when warmth comes at the expense of efficiency, or vice versa. Then, it's a judgment call. One solution involves a Jetsonian compromise: personalizing the technology you use to deliver service. Consider Rosie the Robot, the animatronic housekeeper with a New Yawk accent and an attitude to match; she's not a bad model to follow when designing your customer-facing technology.

Concerns to the Contrary
It can be scary to reconsider the role that human beings play in an organization. Employees, including managers, often reflexively prefer doing things the way they've done them before, allowing habit to replace analysis and creativity. Furthermore, people need jobs, and the easiest ones to provide them with are the ones they've always done, the ones they currently hold. My personal and professional belief is that the best jobs for service employees are the ones that allow them to provide a warm, intelligent human touch where it is needed, and that there should be plenty of such positions to go around, even after routine processes are automated. However, I'm not naïve enough to expect that everyone in every organization will share my vision: Shortsighted bosses and the shareholders they work for will be sorely tempted to offload the transactional and then "forget" to use the resulting bonus—available, motivated workers—to create the kind of personable experiences that build customer engagement and loyalty.

This prospect scares me too. My mission is simple: Improve service, company cultures and employee conditions. I would never want to be confused with someone who advocates that a company do the minimum (or employ the minimum) that it can get away with. But I also recognize that an approach to service that's out of step with customers will ultimately drive an organization's customers—and jobs—elsewhere.

I'm With Stupid

Let's look at something fun and innovative: the Domino's Pizza Tracker. This app and Web-based widget lets you check on the pizza you've ordered at every stage, providing real-time information that relieves anxiety, eliminates wasted phone calls and even provides a bit of levity. (The historian in me notes that the Pizza Tracker replaces Domino's original, spectacularly ill-conceived 30-minute delivery guarantee. That promise proved so dangerous to pedestrians who got in the way of Domino's overtaxed drivers that the company was soon on track to become a full-employment fund for trial lawyers.)

With the Pizza Tracker, the customer enters his phone number and is shown how his order progresses through Domino's five-stage timeline:

1. Order Placed
2. Prep
3. Bake
4. Quality Check
5. Out for delivery

There is logic behind this perhaps frivolous-sounding app. As a customer I don't really care whether my pizza takes 30 minutes or 35 minutes. What I *do* want to know—and the delivery driver may too—is whether I'll have any clothes on when the doorbell rings.

Your ability to keep employees from gumming up the works depends in part on ensuring that customers have everything they need, without needing to ask you for it. In the case of the Pizza Tracker, it's saving customers from ever having to call Domino's to ask "Is my order coming?"/"*When* is it coming?"/"Oh no—I hope I remembered to order my lactose-intolerant girlfriend's half without cheese. Can you double-check for me?" and so forth.

This is how the customer experience today should work. Companies need to learn that it's bad business to wear customers and prospects down by requiring them to spend time and effort to contact your business for what I refer to (with my less squeamish consulting clients at least) as *Stupid Sh-t*™: questions that customers will likely have and that you as a provider should have predicted would come up. (For my profanity-opposed clients, I call this *Stupid St-ff*™, which works about as well.) Customers don't want to call you to find out whether an order has shipped; they want an immediate, automated confirmation by email. And they're similarly peeved when they get lost while trying to visit your office because they had to guess your physical, GPS-friendly address, since only your PO Box is listed on the website. You need to ruthlessly and creatively hunt down these time-wasters yourself for the sake of your customers. Strive to elevate the lowly concept of "avoiding stupid sh-t" to a high art in your organization.

Lowe's, the brick-and-mortar purveyor of bricks and mortar, recently developed MyLowes, an online tool that helps customers retrieve information about previous Lowe's purchases. The tool's functionality allows customers to retrieve warranty information, get targeted tips about using items in their purchase history, reorder items they've purchased before and buy complementary products.[8]

Compare this to asking the Lowe's clerk du jour, "Do you remember that power drill I bought 18 months ago? I need a new screwdriver attachment that will fit it. Sorry, I didn't bring it with me." (Setting up MyLowes wasn't pure-hearted altruism, of course: Enrolling customers in the program also expands Lowe's wealth of data on how customers shop.)

Nate Long, a marketing and PR practitioner who is a millennial himself, tells me, "[We] millennials expect an environment that allows us to serve ourselves for anything trivial, without having to ask." Nate gives a nod to another hardware store, Ace Hardware, for doing this "especially, and surprisingly, well. Ace lays the store out in a way that makes it easy for the customer to navigate their way to making almost any routine purchase on their own"—items intended for use together are grouped intelligently, there's signage that's intelligible to even a very part-time handyman—"yet they have very knowledgeable staff on hand to answer project-specific questions," which is an excellent approach to take in many industries and contexts today.

Ignoring the Jetsons: the Traditional Hotel Check-in Model

Hoteliers have traditionally conceived of check-in as an important moment for high-touch service, rather than as a merely transactional function. They put great stock in finding ways to ensure that the check-in experience is personal and memorable. I, too, am in favor of these hospitable goals; the trouble comes when these goals are pursued at the expense of speed and efficiency, and without giving guests any choice in the matter. Modern hotel guests will inevitably compare the slow, benevolently authoritarian hotel check-in process with the seamless online booking and air travel experience that has just carried them to the hotel's front desk, and they'll likely find the contrast a bit absurd.

Stand in line. Wait for a front desk agent. Orally deliver intricate, intimate information to that agent. Watch him slowly and approximately enter this data on a DOS-era computer terminal, the same data that an average consumer has used for online service transactions six times that same day. Allow the clerk to choose the room, based on only nominal knowledge of the guest's preferences. Wait to be handed a room key, at which juncture the clerk, in a suddenly powerful voice, asks that cringe-inducing question, "How many keys would you like, Ms.____ [last-name-which-I'm-going-to-say-particularly-loud-in-case-somebody-in-the-lobby-wants-to-know-if-you're-expecting-a-visitor]?" Finally, listen to the agent's canned recitation of the hotel's unique features—before you're finally liberated to go about your business.

Hotels would do well to find a way to resolve the check-in conundrum. And some of them are. Hilton has recently announced a smartphone-based check-in solution, for example, and Citizen M, a stylish but "limited service" (cheap) hotel chain in Europe, has entirely eliminated the front desk, replacing it with a bank of self-service check-in kiosks similar to those found in airports. Unlike your average airport, however, Citizen M has a cadre of truly engaging employees working the lobby: "Hi, and welcome. Have you been to Citizen M before? First time? Great, let me help you check in."

Although the employee offers to handle the check-in himself, he also indicates to the guest that the self-service approach is really a snap. True to his word, the kiosk technology is great. Typing in the first few characters of the guest's last name brings up the reservation details. Payment is confirmed with a swipe of the card, and instructions on the screen direct the guest to a box of blank key cards on the counter in front of the kiosk. Tapping on the screen encodes the keycard and a separate receipt pops out with the room number printed on it. All the while, the smartly dressed and eager staff members are nearby and available to help. Fast, efficient and friendly.

Not for Everyone

But the Citizen M model isn't to everyone's taste, nor is it right for every service environment. Says ultra-luxury hotelier Mark Harmon, CEO of Auberge Resorts: "I think the kiosk can come off as offensive, especially when you're paying a few more bucks for your room"—as Harmon coyly puts it; a night at an Auberge property can reach the four digits—"I certainly share the goal of offloading transactional details, just not forcibly offloading them onto the guest."

Harmon prefers to "use a roving iPad to check people in without ever making them wait in line—and [hoteliers should] reconsider if they even *need* to make guests go through check-in at all. We often know our guests and their expected arrival ahead of time, and can welcome them and hand them their keys directly," without either cattle-call queuing or making guests perform the check-in work themselves.

Likewise, when guests arrive at the David Rockwell-designed Nobu Hotel in Las Vegas, they're greeted by a concierge who takes them to their room via a dedicated elevator for a private in-room iPad registration. And at the Andaz in Maui (Andaz is a new, innovative hotel brand from Hyatt), another design from David Rockwell replaces the standard single check-in desk. In Rockwell's words, "Cozy groupings of furniture provide a more welcoming and personal experience: Each individual check-in desk features different, unique touches, such as telescopes or sandpits." Sounds like a well-considered attempt to bring both sides of the Jetsons equation to bear on the check-in situation in appropriate proportions.

Whatever streamlining solution is applied to the check-in experience, once it is instituted the duties of the lobby staff can be redefined. While one staffer handles check-in, another can show guests around the lobby and explain the offerings and hours of the hotel's café and bar. A third can draw a map to a nearby museum or help guests hail a cab. The staff can focus, in other words, on making the guest experience better and more meaningful, instead of on queue control and laborious data entry.

Streamlining Retail

Retail faces a similar problem of using an old model to serve new customers. For retailers, this challenge presents itself most clearly at the end of the customer's experience, when the customer's trying to pay and get out of the store. Let me state what should be obvious: When a customer's trying to hand over her money, she shouldn't be forced to endure a line for the privilege of doing so! Many merchants still fail to understand this, but their customers, who have grown used to the ease of online checkout, are no longer happily queuing up in front of registers in the physical world.

The point here is not just that a tablet can replace a cash register. It's that the whole concept of a separate queuing area, a place set aside intentionally for the customer to wait before being allowed to pay and leave, shouldn't exist. When your customers are shopping online, they're not corralled into a standing formation until the website's ready to check them out—so why should merchants think it's ok to do this to customers in the real world? Nobody appreciates a line except, I suppose, a zebra admiring another zebra during courting season, and today's millennials are no zebras. Their tolerance for lines is "less than minimal," in the words of millennial marketer Nate Long.

It's time for you to abolish queuing and register areas and replace them with a setup that's more fluid and Internet-like to "escape being tied down to the traditional model of a 'cash route,' where you go to a *place* to do the transaction," as retail expert and Accumula Technologies CEO Evan Brubaker puts it.

This is the model with which the Apple Store burst onto the scene, providing an experience where the mechanics of the transaction—receipts, register, cash drawer—are kept out of view, allowing the focus to turn to the customer, the service, the experience. While it may seem ambitious to model yourself on Apple, new tools make a similar approach possible for merchants of most sizes and budgets.

Let's look at how one of these new tools, from Brubaker's Accumula Technologies, a POS (point-of-sale device) specialty company, has improved the customer experience at Camelion Design, a small, seasonally busy home design and accessories retailer in Seattle. For 15 years, Camelion's customers have been served, sometimes with difficulty, by a single cash register. During the holidays, this has historically meant as many as 10 or 15 customers might be stewing in line. Two summers ago, Accumula installed a POS system designed by Lightspeed to remedy the situation. It runs on three Apple devices, allowing any employee anywhere in the store to ring up customers on the spot. Three employees can handle three transactions at once (or more, with the addition of more iPads and employees). Now when the holidays roll around, Camelion never has much of a line at all.

What's more, employees are never taken off the floor as they would be with a register or multiple registers that need to be manned. Taking employees off the floor to staff a register has well-known negative consequences in retail: Sales, service and loss prevention are all likely to be affected.

Improving Choice and Availability

Customers weaned on online shopping not only fail to appreciate lines, they chafe under limitations in choice and availability. Happily, improving options for customers can sometimes be relatively simple to accomplish. As an example, let's look at the booking app that Drybar, a fast-growing, innovative "blowout bar" salon, has developed. If a customer uses the Drybar app to book an appointment for a hair blowout, not only can the customer make an appointment 24/7 (and cancel or reschedule 24/7), but when a desired time isn't available at the client's first salon choice, she's offered that very slot at other nearby Drybar locations, thus expanding the customer's choices and Drybar's availability in one fell swoop.

Emulating Drybar's approach is an effective way to fulfill today's customers' expectations that an "endless inventory" is within grasp, not unlike the raft of options millennials have come to expect from growing up online—the endless inventory of music found on iTunes, movies on Netflix and just about everything on Amazon.

Don't Fence Them In: Customers Want You to Be Omnichannel

Millennials have come of age lacking the sense of limitations in commerce that their elders have long accepted. They don't believe that commerce needs to take place on one channel or operating system (on a desktop browser running Chrome, for example) to the exclusion of another (a tablet running Safari). They will be sure to Yelp your business a new one if you don't honor your online pricing in your store, or if you refuse to honor a gift card in your store that someone sent the customer by email.

What they want is what's called—jargon alert—omnichannel. To put it simply, omnichannel is the future of just about everything that involves extracting money from a customer in a way that they actually *enjoy* having it extracted.

So what does—should—omnichannel look like? Let's take a peek.

On a late, bright Thursday morning, Meghan Millennial is walking down a Washington, DC, sidewalk when her phone buzzes, inviting her into an adjacent store for a cupcake in a flavor she's enjoyed there before. Having just eaten brunch (one of the most important meals of the day), she keeps walking but mentally files the text for later. Half a block later, a Patagonia store catches her eye and she steps in. As she enters the foyer, her phone buzzes again with a coupon for 20% off for the next two hours on dresses. Meghan likes the offer and works with a salesperson to find the right dress. However, the store doesn't have it in her size. No biggie: The salesperson locates it in another store and offers to drop-ship it to Meghan's house. But wait! Meghan now wants two of the dresses, and Patagonia's other location only has one. The salesperson locates one dress in that store and one in a store in Ohio, coordinates the drop-shipping for both, and gives her the BOGO (buy one, get one) discount she deserves (better, after all, than the 20% off that tempted her initially), even though both dresses come from different stores, and neither from the store in which she's standing.

That afternoon, back at home, Meghan finds that three shoeboxes from Macy's have arrived. Two of the pairs fit her perfectly; the third is too tight.

Needing that third style for the weekend, yet dreading the time it'll take to hunt for the item in person, Meghan opens Macy's mobile website on her phone before setting out. She finds the shoes in a better-fitting size and orders them for in-store pickup the next morning, which suits her schedule better than waiting at home. The pickup is ready when she comes in, and with the proximity functionality on her phone, the store's employees are able to recognize her arrival, stop folding clothes and other low-value tasks, and hurry to meet Meghan at the front door—handy, since in grand DC tradition, she's double-parked—where they hand her the package and accept her exchange, wishing her well with an e-coupon to return.

All of the channel-melding that our hypothetical Meghan has just enjoyed can currently be accomplished in retail. It isn't easy for a business to pull off, but customers want and are starting to expect exactly this. Furthermore, customers have little to no understanding of or sympathy for your difficulties in pulling off omnichannel retailing, even though these difficulties are assuredly significant. Your inventory systems and databases need to be connected. Your return procedures and order histories need to be synchronized. While none of this is easy to accomplish, it's easier now than it used to be. Companies like Micros, recently acquired by Oracle, specialize in building systems and technology that allow this coordination. When a customer returns a dress via any channel (ships it back, drops it off in-store, etc.) the merchant's general ledger is adjusted, order history is appended and inventory is updated. So a phone call or Web interaction, even moments after an in-store return, can be based on up-to-the-minute information.

New technology also offers merchants the opportunity to expand inventory beyond what's in front of the customer: Small retailers can use systems such as the Lightspeed solution installed by the above-mentioned Accumula, while larger retailers (such as Macy's) can use the more elaborate systems that Micros and others offer that provide a "show-and-tell" feature with enhanced-resolution photos from multiple angles. This feature allows a customer, while still interacting with a salesperson in-store, to examine in detail items that aren't found on the showroom floor. This expands the store's inventory without requiring the store to commit valuable real estate. And it puts to bed the perennial frustration customers have after schlepping across town to a store only to learn that the desired item is unavailable in the right size/color/fabric.

When this experience becomes truly seamless, truly centered on the customer and her perspective, you've achieved omnichannel. And the benefit to you is more than the pleasant experience you'll be providing your customers, although that's a big part of it. This approach makes the sales process seamless and almost invisible to boot, and by removing barriers to buying you will likely spur customers to purchase more. When you lower the barrier to returning items, perhaps a few more items get returned, but again, you increase present and future sales due to greater customer comfort with the returns process. When you lower the barrier to reaching your company through any possible channel, you'll hear from the customer more—and more often with an open pocketbook.

3

Become a Speed Freak

What your customers expect in terms of speed is growing more extreme every day, accelerating with the pace of technological development. Faster internet speeds, increased access to the Web, the proliferation of smartphones and tablets, intuitive search functions and always-on GPS are some of the developments that influence the timeliness expectations that customers have.

Millennials in particular place a premium on speed and convenience. They're twice as likely as other customers to buy their groceries at convenience stores (in spite of these stores' wild markups), and they disproportionately patronize fast-casual options like Panera, Chipotle and Pei Wei, as well as prepackaged to-go food options—all of which dispense with the waiting-around-for-waitstaff routine. [9]

But millennials are merely the most visible front for these changes: Customers of all ages now expect speedier service, in part because successful brands, both upstarts and established players, have shown it's possible to speed up service without sacrificing quality. This new norm creates a risk that your business will founder by failing to keep up with the accelerated timetable demanded by customers.

Avoiding the Cliff of Dissatisfaction

The cliff of dissatisfaction is the point at which a customer loses faith in the timeliness of your company or your product. The length of time it takes a customer to reach the cliff varies from business to business, but it's a risk inherent in every service interaction and business relationship.

A great business devotes itself to keeping customers safely away from this precipice. Starbucks knows how long an average customer will wait, from acknowledgement ("Can I get something started for you?") to receipt of a finished, customized drink. Starbucks dresses its stores with clever merchandising and appealing décor to make these minutes pass as pleasantly as possible, but it also understands that, ultimately, too long is still not good enough. When "too long" threatens, countermeasures are taken. For example, baristas will venture out from behind their espresso machines to take orders from people who haven't yet reached the counter. Starbucks ultimately lets the cliff of dissatisfaction guide its business expansion. As soon as the company's metrics indicate that the level of demand, and the resulting wait times, are routinely threatening customer satisfaction, Starbucks opens another store down the block.

Casino management is a highly scientific discipline that leaves the gambling solely to its customers. The team at Caesars Entertainment knows how long the average gambler will wait for a complimentary drink on the casino floor before he gets fed up. They know within how many minutes after arrival a casino guest needs to be greeted before he'll wander elsewhere, as well as how many minutes can elapse between subsequent service touches and free drinks without him moving on. Caesars doesn't rely on intuition to guide how it staffs the casino floors; it turns to staff tracking and other data for help. Some operations even sew RFID (radio frequency identification) tags into the uniforms of their cocktail servers—don't ask me where—which are scanned as the waitstaff enter and exit the bar. Managers then track the time a server takes to sweep her section and return to the bar for her customers' orders, data the casino uses to improve its decisions about staffing and flow.

When it comes to your own business, if you harbor a nagging feeling that you haven't been paying enough attention to issues of timeliness, you're probably right. The standards of your entire industry may lag behind the expectations of today's customers. A friend of mine tried to order furniture for his new home recently, only to be told that delivery would take 12 weeks. "Did you *seriously* say twelve weeks?" he shot back in genuine amazement, having never been quoted such a long turnaround for any service or product. But here's the source of the disconnect: Within certain sectors of certain industries, 12 weeks is actually normal. These are industry sectors that haven't felt much motivation to improve, because their direct competitors aren't any better. The thing is, if *everyone* in your industry is too slow, it's time for *you* to be the one to revamp your field before someone—the future Uber, Amazon or Netflix of your industry—does it first.

Want to Outfox Your Competitors? Compress Time

Two hospitals with Midwestern origins—Mayo Clinic and Cleveland Clinic—have become world-famous for their innovative approaches to healthcare. Both hospitals have succeeded in part by challenging the traditional (read: slow) model of medicine. At the Mayo Clinic, patients fly in from all over the world for "efficient, time-compressed care that can usually provide a definitive diagnosis and sometimes initial treatment, including major surgery, within three to five days," as Leonard L. Berry, author of *Management Lessons From Cleveland Clinic,* puts it.

Mayo refuses to settle for the sluggish, unreliable timeline common in many hospitals today. One way Mayo sets itself apart is in its approach to reading scans, such as mammograms. Less time-sensitive hospitals put all scans, whether taken early in the day or late in the afternoon, into a slowly filling holding "basket," then wait until the evening to analyze and interpret them. This means a patient may be called a day later and asked to suffer through a redo (and another torturous round of waiting) if a technical issue arises with the initial scan. Compare this to the procedure at Mayo, where scans are read more or less on the spot, allowing them to be verified while doctors are still at the patient's side.[10]

Ohio-based Cleveland Clinic has itself developed a focus on timeliness, and has used it as an instrument to overcome a historical reputation for patient insensitivity. (Ten years ago, Cleveland Clinic's patient satisfaction scores ranked among the lowest 10% of the nation. Now they're among the world's highest.)

Cleveland Clinic achieved this remarkable transformation by working backward. The clinic began with an "unrealistic" goal and then went to work figuring out how it could be achieved. The goal? Anybody calling the Cleveland Clinic for an appointment, with any specialty, would be seen that same day. Cleveland Clinic's success in pulling this off is quite an accomplishment when you consider it in contrast to the month-long waits some specialists demand their patients endure.

Call Cleveland Clinic today and you'll hear a mind-blowing greeting: "Thank you for calling Cleveland Clinic. Would you like to be seen today?" Only after 4 p.m. does the greeting roll over to "Would you like to be seen tomorrow?"

This commitment to speed comes in part from Cleveland Clinic's awareness of the growing number of millennial patients it sees and whom it expects to see more of as they age and start families of their own. As Dr. James Merlino, who heads Patient Experience for Cleveland Clinic, tells me, "Nobody of any age wants to wait, but we understand that the expectations of the millennial generation are especially accelerated, and this has certainly affected our thinking."

Pulling off the same-day appointment feat has been far from easy. The effort at Cleveland Clinic had to clear some high hurdles. Dr. Merlino says that an extraordinary amount of time and effort are devoted to "managing the flow and ensuring we have the capacity."

A sophisticated triage process is key to the same-day appointment promise. Let's say I call up the clinic and report, "I have a headache. I want to see a neurosurgeon." I'll be taken through a series of questions.

Depending on how I answer them, the agent on the Cleveland Clinic line will determine whom I should see and will ensure I get that same-day appointment.

It's unlikely that I'll see a neurosurgeon for my headache, but I *will* see a headache specialist, or get face or phone time with a nurse who can further assess what I need. On the other hand, says Merlino, "If you call and say, 'Look, I was in [a local] emergency department last night with a headache; they did a CAT scan and say I have a brain tumor. I need to be seen by a neurosurgeon today,' you *will* see that neurosurgeon today. Or if you call in with a headache [and] you say certain things which are warning signs—answering yes to 'is this the worst headache you ever have in your life?' is one—you will immediately be transferred to a nurse who will do more assessment and then guide you to our emergency department."

In healthcare and other professional fields, timeliness is key because so often the conclusions to be drawn from professional services are complex and/or ambiguous. It can be exceedingly difficult for laymen (in this case, the patient and his loved ones) to tell what qualifies as a "good" result for any particular condition or situation. In medicine, is a lengthy but ultimately full recovery a good outcome or a bad one considering the particulars of the case? It's hard to tell sometimes. For legal clients, it's similar: When a lawsuit goes to court (which you'd think would be an area where results are cut and dried), is paying out a settlement of X dollars a good outcome? Or, considering the strength of the case with which you entered the courtroom, should you feel like you've been taken to the cleaners? Again, it's hard for a client to tell. In such technically complex situations, efficiency and speed are often used as proxies by customers to judge overall quality and care.

Audit the Timeliness of Your Own Business

If you want to improve your company's timeliness, conduct an informal audit yourself, taking the perspective of a customer, in order to suss out how closely you're meeting their needs. I suggest four parts to this quick test.

1. **Anyone there?** First, submit an inquiry via one of your site's webforms. How quickly does someone respond to your inquiry? 18 hours? 36? Such a lag may have been fine within the languid commercial landscape of 2003, but an 18-hour response time feels like *years* in Internet time today. Your customer may have already moved on before you get around to responding. Even if they haven't, the impression you've left is less than stellar.

2. **Try to get the info you need.** A second test involves trying to gather some simple but important information from your company without interacting with a human: facts such as hours of operation (including upcoming holiday weekends), GPS coordinates for drivers and file formats that your company will accept for uploads—the information your customers will likely search for on your site. Don't phone, don't email. Just look for this info from easily available sources, such as your site's FAQ page. More often than not, you'll find the information is either unavailable or incomplete.

3. **Promises, promises.** Now, check what happens when someone from your company—or an automated message from your computers—makes a promise to a customer. Does your company keep that promise? Do your packages ship when you said they would? Are the items listed as in stock actually in stock? Does your receptionist arrive at 9 a.m. as your website promises? Furthermore, do you err on the side of the customer? For example, if your company sends out a service technician with a promise of arrival "between the hours of 1 and 3 p.m.," does the technician show up at 2:55, thus technically meeting the deadline but inconveniencing your customer for the remainder of the afternoon?

4. **If a complaint falls in the forest ...** Finally, check what happens when you post a complaint or concern online. (Yes, it's your company, so you'll want to keep the posted complaint minor and delete it once the experiment's done.) In far too many cases, *nothing* happens. Or nothing will happen for far too long. This doesn't cut it for customers, who want to be reassured that their voices are

being heard, particularly when they voice concern or displeasure. Furthermore, many customers have an expectation of a real-time or nearly real-time relationship with your company, particularly through social media. If you're on Twitter or Facebook and a disappointed or aggrieved customer posts something on your page or directs a tweet to your company, he expects your company will see it and respond. Nothing makes a complaint worse than having it fester. And there's almost no response to a compliment that's more disheartening than having it languish unacknowledged. Forging a relationship with your customer means responding quickly to your customer's attempts to reach out—no matter how inconvenient the timing may be.

Real-Time Is the Right Time for Customer Support

A recent customer service initiative at Google offers a lesson in the power of real-time customer support.

Google's customer service used to be something of a farce. Slothlike and equivocating, Google's sketchy customer support was historically the price a business paid to be an advertising customer of Google's powerful AdWords program. But times have changed: The company has doubled its customer satisfaction scores from 44% to 90% by moving almost all its Google's customer support interactions from a wait-for-response model to real-time. [11]

In the past, if you needed Google's help with your advertising account, you'd send an email (the only channel of support Google offered) and receive a reply maybe 10 to 16 hours later. And this initial answer was never satisfying. Sometimes you'd just get a "Dear Advertising Customer, in order to assist you, we need to know more" kind of response, demanding some technical detail you'd neglected to put in your initial email 16 hours earlier. Once you then provided this missing, often picayune bit of information, you then would wait *another* 16 hours for what still might be an incomplete answer to your question.

In 2010 and earlier, "you basically could just email us, and that was it," concedes Deepak Khandelwal, the Google vice president who led the charge to improve. So Khandelwal replaced the email-and-wait routine with enough phone and live-chat support that wait times now range from zero to 30 seconds for calls and chats (in the 42 languages in which Google provides advertiser support).

Google's example demonstrates that it's not necessary to make customers languish in a state of worry and growing frustration. They don't have to be forced to solve their own problems with incomplete information, or sit through a lengthy piecemeal support process. Most of all, there's no need for the situation to escalate due to customers' feelings of impotence as the lag time between query and response grows. The real-time model prizes customers' time and helps them right when they need help—now.

4

Build Something Genuine

Today's customers have a well-developed sense of what is and isn't genuine and an advanced ability to spot corporate hogwash. To win customers over today, a business—its leaders, frontline workers, marketers and behind-the-scenes operators—needs to behave in a way that is genuine and is perceived by customers to be authentic.

Few customers of any age are fond of artifice, but the search for what's genuine is particularly emblematic of the millennial generation. Previous generations, unsatisfied with and rebelling from their homes of origin, have also searched for authenticity: Picture the upper-crust young lady leaving home to "[meet] a man from the motor-trade," in Lennon and McCartney's "She's Leaving Home." But as a generational trait, this search for what's authentic is especially pronounced in millennials, the theme having emerged from a confluence of factors better dissected by a sociologist than me: a childhood interrupted by 9/11, the collapse of traditionally rock-solid institutions during and following the 2008 economic meltdown, the stylistic influence of reality TV and hand-held YouTube videos, and the eye-level communicative, educational and parenting styles with which they've grown up.

How to Exude "Genuine"
Some of what creates authenticity is intrinsic to your brand: your origins (for example, being first or storied in a particular marketplace: Levi's, Sam Adams and so forth), a genuine founder or spokesperson who personifies authenticity

(Yvon Chouinard, the climber/founder of Patagonia, to name one standout) and similar factors that might feel beyond your control. But some genuine elements of a brand—the elements with which this book is concerned—can be consciously created as part of the overall customer experience. The keys to projecting a genuine brand reside in the cues you are giving about your image through the customer experience you create, and here's where you have an opportunity to transform doing business from a generic and perhaps suspect exchange into something meaningful for your customers, something that attracts their continuing and increasing business over time.

Genuineness, as it applies to the service experience, is conveyed through:

- *Language:* word choice and scripting (or lack thereof)
- *Service style:* an eye-level, peer-to-peer, non-servile communication style and an appropriate level of formality, including how employees dress and identify themselves
- *Visual, tactile and sensory clues:* design, materials, finishes and furnishings

Genuine Language and Communication

Customers in today's marketplace favor a straightforward, down-to-earth, even slangy style of communication from most types of business professionals with whom they interact. (Some exceptions include oncologists, pilots, accountants and funeral directors.) When it comes to communication, customers today and younger customers in particular are "disillusioned by anything canned and artificial," as business and marketing expert Andrew Jensen puts it. A stilted, overly formal service style, even from the most caring providers, puts a ceiling on how intimate and inviting the interactions can be between employees and customers.

Excessive formality is hazardous to your business because it clashes with the personal style of your customers, millennials in particular, making your brand appear out of touch or even condescending. For example, traditionally prescribed hospitality language has included the use of phrases like "my pleasure" and "certainly, Sir," which work up to a point but sound wooden when overused or used inappropriately. "It was really my pleasure to visit with you during your stay, Mr. Jamison" is fine, but never: "It will be my pleasure to clean your toilet." [12]

A good way to enforce reasonable language standards, without hobbling the verbal footwork of your employees, is what I've named the Danny Meyer Method, after the great New York restaurateur. With the Meyer Method, although you ask your employees to nix certain phrases ("it's our policy," "to be honest with you," "uh-huh," "you guys," or this pet peeve of Danny's: "Are *we* still *working* on the lamb?"), you don't prescribe specific replacements, leaving that up to the creativity and individuality of your staff. This approach has the additional benefit of keeping your employees comfortable in their own skins, using their own shorthand as needed with customers. You're providing employees with boundaries in their interactions but empowering them by letting them use their own style within those parameters.

Dare to Go Scriptless

In almost all settings, I suggest doing away with word-for-word scripts but retaining a "punch list" of points that need to be covered in the course of a conversation. (Life-and-death settings such as healthcare and pharmaceutical delivery are important exceptions, as are interactions that have privacy or security implications.) This approach to customer interactions avoids running into customers' innate dislike of being read to from a script.

Let's look again at Drybar, the blow-dry-and-style salon phenomenon that has transformed the hair care landscape in just a couple of years. The Drybar customer experience is extraordinarily well thought out, made up of hundreds of carefully created touchpoints that make the experience memorable for its customers. And it all happens without a script. At no point in its operation, explains cofounder Michael Landau, does Drybar "train to a script, though in our contact center we give [agents] a lot of prompts they should hit on the phone—to ask about [the customer's] hair length and other such details," because checking in about these details directly improves the experience once the customer arrives at Drybar. "Because our growth has been so fast"—when I first became aware of Drybar in 2010, it had four shops, all in Southern California; as of this writing it's up to nearly 40 salons across the U.S., with London opening soon—"we think a lot about how, as we grow, we will manage to convey to customers and to employees that they are part of a business with the spirit of a smaller, more flexible company." The refusal to script allows Drybar to maintain this flexible, genuine feeling in two ways: It provides a less stilted experience and it builds more empowered and flexible employees to serve customers, thanks to the leeway that Drybar is providing these employees.

Drybar isn't providing or enforcing a script, but its leaders have laid out guidelines that its contact center employees need to heed to ensure a successful booking and blowout session, in other words a carefully plotted framework for ensuring their customers are properly cared for. While training and monitoring are needed to ensure these intakes are executed properly, this isn't scripting. And it *couldn't* be successfully scripted because high-quality service requires employees to tailor their approach to the quirks of a particular customer in a given context. Scripting, on the other hand, is "dependent on your customer following a script himself," as contact-center expert Colin Taylor puts it; it only works if customers behave in an expected pattern to which you can respond with a predetermined line. But customer concerns come in infinite varieties, with infinite moods, paces and nuances.

So instead of training to a script, the best thing an organization can do is teach its people to deal with situations, both good and difficult. Give them the tools to recognize behaviors and respond appropriately and effectively. Or as Doug Carr of FRHI Hotels & Resorts (Fairmont, Raffles and Swissotel are their brands) puts it, "The things that matter can't be scripted. You can build scenarios for your staff, but you need to couple this with encouragement and training for your staff on how to read the customer, and then doing what's right and what's appropriate."

Sara Kearney of Hyatt puts it like this, "It takes an awful lot of practice to come across as completely unscripted ... We don't script [at Hyatt's brand, Andaz], but we do an awful lot of role plays and dress rehearsals to help people understand their role in bringing the brand experience to life."

Departing from formula isn't easy. (Easy would be prescribing specific words for an unempowered employee to read.) But the results are worth it, and the impact will be clear in the flexible, nuanced, genuine brand of service you offer.

Eye-Level Peer-to-Peer Communication

Boomer parents by and large avoid talking down to their children, from shunning baby talk when the children were young to including older children in family discussions and decisions, say marketers and generational thinkers Joeri Van den Bergh and Mattias Behrer. This approach is also true, generally, of the schoolteachers who educated these millennials as they grew up. It was even true for the hosts-cum-stars of the most influential television shows from millennials' childhood, from Joe and Steve on *Blue's Clues* to Bob and Wendy on *Bob the Builder*, as I discussed earlier.

So should a company stand loftily above its customers, putting on a snobby accent à la the classic ads for Grey Poupon? Not if it wants to have a successful commercial relationship with today's customers. A company should instead aspire to communicate on a level plane with today's customers, as a peer, in other words. Your marketing department would do well to consider this. (Even Grey Poupon's marketers have cleverly updated their messaging of late with a more winking sensibility about its high-class airs.) It also has interesting implications for how service should be delivered: What I call "service style."

A young traveler recently described to me a service encounter she enjoyed:

"I was in a Melbourne hotel coffee shop a few months ago. I remember fondly the high-level, intelligent, mutually respectful conversation I had there with the barista. He seemed on a par with me, and my feeling was that we enjoyed each other as a result. By 'on a par,' I guess I mean he seemed not removed from the realities of my life; we were social equivalents even though he was pouring the coffee and I was paying him to pour it. It was comforting—and comfortable."

She went on to rail against a different service style she has encountered, a passive-aggressive version of servility where employees lapse into a stylized simulation of hospitality rather than actually being helpful:

"The best thing a business can do for me is to have an abundance of good staff: eager, of course, but also skilled, effective—like the Geniuses at the Apple Store—and empowered to fix stuff for me. Warm bodies everywhere who can't do anything for me except give me a forced smile? Not what I'm looking for as a customer."

Our young traveler has hit on something important, the idea that businesses do well by encouraging their employees to act more like peers of their customers, less like servants and decidedly not servile. You want employees to project the attitude that everyone is in this together, the server and the served.

Take a moment and picture the great department stores of the past: Marshall Field and the rest; the grand hotels—tea at The Plaza and so forth; the white-gloved, French-accented, towel-over-the-arm restaurants. This model of service, design and atmosphere doesn't really resonate with millennials. It's too imperious and stifling, too mothball-scented. It's also a bit nerve-wracking for the customer, something that service designer Tim

Miller discussed with me: "It's time to get away from the old style of service, where the guest and the employees are always sort of expected to be on their best behavior—like when you're going out with your grandparents. Because that's not the feeling customers are looking for in service at any price point today."

Rethinking Dress Codes, Uniforms, Tattoos and Piercings

By and large, the most successful sartorial approach to take is to encourage your customer-facing employees to dress more or less like your customers (at least like your customers dress on their non-sweatpants days). This puts your customers as well as your employees at ease, and will pay dividends down the road. As is true with language, if you let employees have a choice in what they wear, while still providing them with appropriate boundaries, it can help employees feel more at ease at work, which is exactly what you want if you're aiming for authentic, eye-to-eye communication.

Employees at Andaz Hotels select and purchase their own "uniforms." These uniforms are actually any outfit that catches the employee's eye as long as it is selected from a particular designer's line. This local designer represents the vibe of the hotel's surrounding community. Employees buy the clothes off the rack to fit their own shape and size. (Yes, they're reimbursed—that was the first thing I asked!) What I find smart and encouraging about the Andaz approach is that it puts a premium on looking genuine for guests and making employees *feel* genuine as they go about their duties. Says Sara Kearney from Hyatt, Andaz's parent, "Part of the reason we decided to do this is that oftentimes, when you are looking at buying uniforms for so many different shapes and sizes of employees, actual uniforms may not feel right to an employee. But if they are able to go choose their own clothes, it becomes a positive part of their feeling on the job, that sense of 'I'm wearing my own clothes.'"

The tattoo taboo is an important related issue. Are you reluctant to (or do your hiring guidelines prohibit you to) employ otherwise qualified candidates with visible tattoos, bold hair colors, cheek piercings and the like? Well, I suggest you get over it, for two reasons. First, letting employees revel in their own style of grooming and self-decoration allows your company to project how genuine you are as a brand to employees and to the customers they support. Your customers—including millennials—project their own style through tattoos, piercings and interesting hairstyles, and for the most part, they're fine with your employees doing the same. As customer experience designer Tim Miller puts it, "strive for a visible symbiosis between the people working at your establishment because it fits their lifestyle, and the customers doing business with you because it fits *their* lifestyle."

The second reason is even more important and is memorably personified by a front-of-house service professional in Bermuda named Nick DeRosa. Head doorman at the Fairmont Southampton and one of the greatest front-of-house employees you'll ever meet, DeRosa sports a gigantic tattoo on his neck, in all capital letters, that proclaims "NICK" so visibly his actual name tag serves as mere decoration rather than identifier. Based on an appearance checklist, Nick would hardly be considered a good candidate to be the first person to encounter guests at this grand luxury hotel, yet Fairmont placed him there anyway based on his personality and smile. It's clear that hiring Nick was one of the best personnel decisions the hotel has ever made, because of the service he provides to guests and the inspiration he gives to other front-of-house employees at the hotel. So I hold the example of DeRosa out to you and ask you this: Why lose a potentially great service person who made a questionable (to you) stylistic choice earlier in his life?

You may get some pushback from naysayers citing studies showing that, all things being equal, a tattoo-less, un-pierced employee will be viewed more favorably by mainstream customers than one decorated with ink or piercings. But all things are *never* equal. All employees are not equal. And I would argue that you should employ the tattooed employee if the tattooed employee can be groomed into a future star for your business.

Employees with the potential for greatness all share key personality traits (warmth, empathy, teamwork, conscientiousness and optimism [WETCO] make up my list), but what they don't share is a particular look. As an employer, you dream of great employees. Not necessarily Darien-bred or Oxbridge-accented employees (sometimes these are the employees you want to avoid in the service industry, if they come with an attitude to match), but employees who can be empathetic and creative as they work with customers. That's what makes greatness.

Look, Bro, No Nametag!

As you spec out your future-friendly service style, one item that should be up for discussion is whether you really need nametags in your business, even if it's the norm in your industry. If you're delivering a high-volume, less rarefied offering ("I'm Jayden R., and I'll be taking care of you folks tonight"), name tags are probably on the whole a positive. They promote easy, superficial conversations with customers, and they certainly promote accountability for the employees.

But name badges aren't a hallmark of high-quality service any more than scripted encounters are. While nametags, like scripting, can make trivial interactions easy, they implicitly cap the level of intimacy that a customer is likely to achieve with an employee or the brand the employee represents. If you're handed the employee's first name with no effort on your part as a customer, it allows you to converse with them with little effort, but you probably won't get any further than that zero-effort conversation.

Furthermore, nametags look artificial and forced. Service designer Tim Miller gives this as his reason for doing away with nametags: "We want to avoid the stilted awkwardness of 'look, I work here, I'm taking care of you because that's what it says on my badge I do.'" Other thoughtful service professionals I've recently spoken with agree for the same reason: They are striving to create more of a peer-to-peer and less of a servile or artificially divided relationship.

And boy do employees tend to hate nametags. The irony here is that the right to wear a personal badge stating one's last name was a hard-won victory for travel-industry employees in a landmark case. The porters on George Pullman's railroad (all of them black men) were, in a breathtaking display of racism, universally referred to by passengers as "George," regardless of their actual name, leading them to demand and ultimately win the right to have name badges with their own last name on them. Yet the current feeling among employees I've interviewed is that a name badge tends to be used by their more obnoxious customers not as a tool to strike up better conversation but as leverage that allows them to threaten trouble via Yelp, TripAdvisor or a complaint to the manager.

What Today's Customers Hate in Design: Gilded Ceilings, Ostentation, Car-Centricity

Look around you at the most emotionally satisfying designs and furnishings today in retail, restaurants, hotels and offices. These designs contrast sharply with what prevailed in high-end commercial design until about a decade ago: extreme gilding and ostentatious ornamentation, and—more recently—ultra-stark, cold minimalism, where humans almost look out of place. Now, in a happier evolution, great designers, decorators and landlords today have started spending money differently. They're creating commercial spaces that fit the new generation and zeitgeist better. This translates to a use of materials that don't look as polished as their forebears: a preponderance of hemp, handmade tiles and rough-hewn elements where the "hand" of the artisan still shows in the work and human imperfections are a part of the appeal. [13] This fits a common, if not universal, move away from ostentation among today's customers. Even the wealthier among the millennial generation steer away from being identified with the "1%." Overall, there's less aspiration toward a life of wealth and ostentation for its own sake, including a growing reluctance to buy cars as status symbols. (One possible sociological explanation? The global financial crisis they witnessed firsthand and whose wake continues to shake them. Experiencing the havoc that mindless greed can unleash has increased millennials' skepticism about the permanence and meaningfulness of raw materialism.)

Young travelers and the more on-trend among their elders are put off by gratuitous status symbols such as gold leaf, crystal chandeliers, incongruously located Corinthian columns, and ostentatiously staged Bentleys and Rolls-Royces in front of hotel entrances. They're troubled by these cues just as they are by excessive formality and servility in service style and dress. These cues summon up another era, one that doesn't reflect the economic realities they've had to face. Gussy up your establishment with these would-be luxuries and a millennial's reaction will be, "Am I in the wrong place?"

Yes to Quirky, No to Cookie Cutter

In design and materials, authenticity can be achieved by doing everything you can to embody the quirks, locale and specificity of a business and its proprietor in the spaces a business shares with its customers. As commercial/hospitality/office/set designer David Rockwell puts it, "We're moving away from commodified environments to more individual places to welcome the emergent millennials. Millennials aren't interested in one-size-fits-all design. They want spaces with distinct personalities that fit whatever one's character, mood or perception of one's self is: hip, quiet, sophisticated, edgy or fun."

To be forward-looking in retail, food service, hospitality and even office environments, you need to understand that ostentation will backfire, even if you're trying to convey a luxe sensibility. Rely instead on proportion, good taste, uncluttered design and the right materials. Aim for a strong sense of place constructed with real materials that age well and create a timeless look that sets customers at ease.

To truly commit to high-quality service, incorporate your eye-level, peer-to-peer approaches when designing your space. Andaz Hotels has designed its public spaces with "barrier-free" environments in mind. (N.B:

When using the term "barrier-free" in this context, Andaz isn't specifically talking about accessible design for people with disabilities.) The Andaz approach to design means guests are no longer separated from staff by a barrier. They now stand or sit side by side with the guest or hold a handheld device in front of the guest where both can see it.

These tweaks may sound minor or even trivial, but according to Sara Kearney from Andaz's parent, Hyatt, the hotel "started to see people's behaviors change immediately; it was really fascinating." Continues Kearney: "I remember sitting in the London hotel lobby for a week where all we did was move to different spots in the lobby and watch the way people reacted when they realized that they were standing side by side with the person who was serving them. It created a little bit more of a peer-to-peer relationship. The feeling was like you're arriving more at a friend's home."

Mark Harmon from Auberge Resorts is even more emphatic: "Customers have a visceral Pavlovian reaction when they walk up to a high desk with employees lined up behind it. They just instantly feel like they're going to get hammered. Get people out from behind the desk. Bring the desk down to a normal desk height if you have to have a desk, but really engage the customer directly—go to the customer (instead of the other way around) and make it personal."

In retail, bringing the checkout to the customer and keeping sales professionals constantly circulating rather than tethered to a register achieves a similar effect. With the tablet-based retail solutions discussed in the previous chapter, salespeople and customers can review details of an order and the options involved together. This side-by-side approach is a solid if subtle step toward more genuine relationships with customers.

5

Your Customer's the Star

Earlier, I urged you to identify and offload any service tasks that can be better done electronically than by hand. This Jetsonian approach, however, can be a magnet for mischief. Once you've saved resources by automating tasks and services, it's tempting to pocket the savings and call it a day. But improving automated customer service is no excuse to offer lousy human-powered service. Instead, take the resources you've recouped through digitization and focus them on meaningful human interactions.

JD Power recently confirmed the importance of personal service in a study of the hospitality industry, in which Power found that the number of employees with whom a guest interacts affects the guest's overall satisfaction. Customers who interact more often with service staff, and with a broader cross-section of that staff, reported greater satisfaction. (The highest satisfaction was reported by guests who were served by four or more types of employees and the lowest by those who received no further service beyond front desk check-in.)

Jiffy Lube may not spring to mind when it comes to exceptional service with a human touch. But the oil-change and automotive-services chain has improved its service model by offloading transactional details that had previously preoccupied their employees and customers, rolling out an intricate nationwide database to store each customer's vehicle history and manufacturer-prescribed service requirements. This information is now a couple of clicks away for every customer-facing Jiffy Lube employee, freeing them from onerous paperwork and allowing them to assist customers more easily and knowledgeably.

At Apple Stores, a relentless effort to downplay transactional items and processes (you'll find no registers, receipts or owner's manuals in sight) leaves the stores uncluttered and the employees empowered to provide a peerless retail experience. Apple has invested in training a large team of salespeople and customer service representatives to help customers on the floor and at the Genius Bar, where the diagnostic specialists are famously called "Geniuses." (Notice how this playful title avoids describing a transactional role and focuses on ability instead.) Apple didn't pocket the savings that it realized by streamlining service. It invested them in the human element.

Now that technology and revamped processes can nudge front desks, long lines and confusing paperwork out of the way, it's time to position your business as more than a throughway for getting your customers, figuratively or literally, from point A to point B. Focus on creating an experience customers can enjoy along the way.

Millennials Are Looking for an Experience

For all the millennial generation's vaunted tech savvy, they're hardly a bunch of cold, analytical Spocks. As marketing consultant Andrew Jensen puts it, "It's a dangerous mistake to think of the millennial generation as hard-edged technocrats. On the contrary, this generation craves personal experiences." Jennifer Fox, president of Fairmont Hotels & Resorts, agrees. Younger customers coming into the marketplace hope and desire that "[we] will deliver an emotional narrative that resonates with them."

Take business travel. Millennials "tend to view business travel not as a necessary evil but as a perk and an opportunity to view the world," as Jay Coldren, VP of Marriott's innovative EDITION Hotels, puts it. The fact that many of them have yet to set down roots (recessions will do that to you!) means that they're less wedded to the notion of home, and more open to travel as an adventure and opportunity. Simply put, they're looking for an experience when they travel, even if they're doing it on the company dime. Supporting this worldview—crafting an immersive, unforgettable experience—can win you their business.

How Drybar Makes a Movie for Its Clients

Think of this experiential approach as giving your customer a chance to star in a movie. At first glance, Drybar should have no business charging $40 for a blowout that anyone could at least approximate at home. But for that $40 premium, it's clear the company is offering much more than meets the eye, judging from Drybar's runaway success. Women (over 100,000 each month) visit a Drybar and return week after week because they feel that their hour at Drybar offers a delightful experience, an elaborate movie that Drybar has created for them to star in.

As co-owner Michael Landau, who started the business with his sister Alli Webb, describes it: "What we're selling at Drybar is a feeling and an experience. For 45 minutes you get to relax and be pampered, drinking a mimosa and indulging in the guilty pleasure of the latest chick flick or celebrity magazine while someone washes and brushes your hair."

Making this metaphorical movie is much like making a real film. It's an involved, often technically complex business. Continuity, casting, lighting and more must be perfected or the illusion falls apart. Film directors such as Christopher Nolan, James Cameron and Peter Jackson spend endless hours poring over shots, making sure the light is just so, that the arch of the lead's eyebrow rises in concert with the rhythm of the background music. Countless minor details merge into a completely immersive experience. It's not a stretch to say that Drybar thinks similarly about how all of the details coalesce in each new salon it opens—subtle touches derived, Landau says, "from our own intuition and experience as well as the feedback we gather from our clients and stylists."

Drybar's craft and professionalism reveal themselves time and again as the "movie" progresses. There's the swift, seamless online booking process and the expert, convivial pre-blowout consultation. Telephone hold times are tracked and kept to a minimum. The menu of blowout styles to choose from is humorously crafted and unique. Each chick flick Drybar screens has been carefully vetted (after all, a good rom com is hard to find) and captioned with subtitles to prevent auditory overload. The salon's music playlist is so distinctive that Drybar has successfully released it as a CD. And Drybar isn't afraid to defy expectations or long-held traditions: Clients don't sit in front of mirrors (until they're wheeled around for the signature "reveal" at the end) because cofounder Webb discovered that clients relax more and micromanage the process less when they're not looking at still wet, not-yet-perfectly-coiffed hair mid-blowout. There are also the branded "Rain Blows" umbrellas that the company gives every client whenever the weather turns stormy. Not to mention the decor, lighting, stemware and chairs. (Drybar tried and tested dozens of different fabrics before agreeing on a chair.) The blow dryers themselves have been smartly tweaked; in an especially filmic touch, Drybar has figured out how to attenuate the sound of its blow dryers, to keep them from roaring like lawnmowers and drowning out the rest of the activity "on set."

Drybar's Landau believes that "the experience is everything—if it weren't for the experience we create, we would just be another place styling women's hair." This experience—the movie—is what has kept knockoffs at bay, despite a business model that looks like a sitting duck for any competitor with a hairdryer, a sink and some forearm strength.

Aim for Enchantment

The movie you'll want to create will vary depending on the nature of your business and, of course, on your particular customer. But if you're looking for a one-word review to summarize a successful customer experience, "enchanting" is a good adjective to aim for. Drybar's clientele are enchanted by all the thoughtful, friendly touches, from the playlist to the cocktails to the umbrellas. At Five Guys Burgers and Fries, customers (the nonallergic ones) are charmed by the throwback imagery of peanuts in brown bags. Enchantment comes when you transport a customer to a place of purpose and vision.

Consider the Mayo Clinic, the integrated medicine mecca in the unlikely Minnesota town of Rochester that I introduced earlier. Mayo chooses to situate its children's cancer center right in the middle of one of its newest buildings (just off the lobby) because Mayo feels this makes the statement that it isn't hiding from this oft-dreaded ailment; it's confronting it head-on. The lighting at Mayo's hospitals is a far cry from traditional hospitals' unnatural fluorescence. It subtly warms the walls and incorporates outside light wherever possible. Mayo incorporates an extra layer of soundproofing in its building plans, mindful that experiences form from all five senses.[14]

All of this puts the patient—"the needs of the patient," as Mayo's motto puts it—at the center of the experience. Through all the pain, fear and uncertainty of a serious illness, this comfort and attention is in its own way enchanting.

Whether lighthearted as at Drybar or serious as at Mayo Clinic, "experiences are the luxuries that today's customers are seeking," says veteran resort operator Mark Harmon. "Whether they're young and looking for adventure and excitement, or older and checking off a bucket list, more and more I find customers want to learn, experience, take part in something. They want to be able to come back and say, 'You know, I *did* that. I was there for this adventure. I did something that not everyone gets to do.'"

Jennifer Fox, the Fairmont Hotels and Resorts president, agrees and raises an interesting point about customers wanting to come home improved: "More than ever, guests want to walk away with a new skill or a heightened level of awareness. [Our] research indicates that younger generations [are looking for us to offer] experiences and amenities that are engaging and educational, while also reflective of the destination."

And the more engaging and surprising the movie you put them in, the more your customers will want to talk about your business. Posting about PDT (Please Don't Tell)—the East Village speakeasy that you enter through a phone booth—is cool. Posting that you're in a banquet hall at the local chain hotel outpost isn't going to have that cachet, or news value. It's nothing to write home about, as the expression puts it, and so they won't.

Nor will many passengers tweet excitedly about flying United or American, as that's hardly a badge of honor. On the other hand, people love to tell their friends they're flying Virgin America because the company has staked its claim on providing an experience that's worth talking about, an approach that gives the airline a clear competitive advantage. The details create a story that people want to retell: purple lighting, wildly catchy dance-based safety videos, abundant TV options, leather seats, great waiting rooms and the "Here on Biz" app that lets you meet other passengers with similar interests. These details make people talk, tweet, post and write about Virgin, because of the distinction and immersion of the experience—the movie—that Virgin has invited them to star in.

6

Set the Stage for Customer Relationships

Let's talk about travel. Remember the old step-by-step sequence? First, plan your itinerary, save up enough money. Then, go on the trip and shoot a few rolls of film along the way. Only then would you involve your friends—or at least try. You'd develop your film into slides (slides!) and strong-arm every friend you could find to come over and watch a carousel worth of your memories, a few of them inserted upside-down.

Travel today no longer has a clear before, during and after. It's all "during," and the "during" is spent with your friends and loved ones, wherever in the world they may be. Friends are, in a sense, always along for the ride: kibitzing, advising and being advised by you as they plan their own trips while you're taking yours. Boston Consulting Group has attempted to quantify this: "For a four-day leisure trip, the average consumer spends 42 hours online ... dreaming about, researching, planning and making reservations, and then sharing their experiences while they travel or when they get back home."

What's true for travel is true in most other commercial arenas. It holds for retail, where girlfriends share selfies from the dressing room so offsite friends can help with fit and style. In dining, customers share course-by-course photos of their meals ("foodographs") in real time. In live entertainment, fans attend concerts and switch perspectives throughout, between the unmediated live experience and viewing or streaming it on their video camera's tiny screen. Even in healthcare, tweets and status updates from inside the ER are not unheard of, notably from professional athletes who suffer serious game-time injuries. Getting medical opinions from offsite friends and family members before and even during some procedures is far from rare to boot.

This is a multigenerational phenomenon. Even the venerable Silent Generation has long moved on from shooting slides and loading them into carousels, often due to the influence of their younger, more tapped-in family members. Customers today of all ages shop, dine and travel socially, thanks in no small part to smartphones. Other technological factors include customers' now-effortless ability to share their experiences and reviews on sites like Yelp and TripAdvisor, as well as the ease of organizing friends, families and unaffiliated interest groups online in ways that result in real-life meetups, dinners, dates, drinks and events.

This socialization of consumption extends beyond those who are traditionally considered friends. Even ostensible strangers—online followers and brands' online reviewers—are in many cases trusted by younger customers more than they trust information that comes directly from even well-established brands, according to Joeri Van den Bergh and Mattias Behrer. Customers today live and consume in a world of search and social. People look for authority online and from acquaintances with similar experiences, perspectives and backgrounds. This leads to quite a shift in how customers end up making their buying decisions. Buyers include their circle of acquaintances, both the physical and virtual kinds, in practically all their commercial activities—which has a real effect on what ends up getting purchased, and how it ends up being experienced.

You're Not the Center of Your Customer's World

To build brand value today, it helps to focus on consumption in a social context. Some new, highly successful businesses—GoPro, which makes a video camera that you can take virtually anywhere, even miles up in the atmosphere like Felix Baumgartner did, is a business built for social sharing—have become wildly valuable because they situate their business around online socialization and sharing. For the rest of us, who offer more traditional services and products, there's one concept I want you to keep in mind, which will help ensure success today, regardless of your product or service: *You're not the center of your customer's world.*

While your business may be the star of *your* life, for your customers it represents something different. A business often insinuates itself best into a customer's life, memory and loyalty by being a backdrop to the story of their lives, as experienced with their friends and family. Restaurants, for example, provide the setting for marriage proposals, love affairs, breakups, arguments and, according to every mob drama I've ever enjoyed, the occasional professional hit. Not to mention the more prosaic: business meetings, shared sunsets and outings with coworkers. This isn't isolated to foodservice settings. Airlines, hospitals, even the DMV can stage the drama that runs through customers' lives. To be successful, service businesses must give guests enough leeway to allow them to live out the thrill and fantasy of their lives with the people who matter to them.

If you take the stage-setting idea seriously, you can expand it in ways that can do wonders for your brand. Hotel 1888 in Sydney, better known as the "Instagram Hotel," facilitates social sharing throughout its customer experience, with predetermined "selfie spaces" and an "Instagram walk" that they've mapped out for you. By celebrating the role of the hotel and its environs as a backdrop, 1888 makes sure it gets in the picture as well.

Take On the Goals of Others

"My goal in life is to make you a hero to your spouse," luxury hotelier Mark Harmon tells me. If Harmon were more shortsighted, he might set his aims on something more conventional: making his hotels the most profitable properties in the luxury hotel market, for example. But Harmon focuses on his customers' goals rather than his own. As he puts it, "The touches we add [help] make for a memorable time together here. This is important, and we take it seriously. In the big scheme of things, how often as a couple do you really—I mean really—get away from the kids and get to connect, in a stress-free setting? We're honored that guests let us be the setting for that, whether or not it's technically what you'd call a special occasion." Harmon feels his Auberge Resorts' success is built upon the relationships his guests have with each other while enjoying Auberge's service. It's an astute and effective way to serve today's customers.

For the fraught, high-stakes referral healthcare that Mayo Clinic is known for, treatment often becomes a socially complex, multigenerational affair. Mayo addresses the inclusion of family members and loved ones through design. Every exam room is designed to encourage collaboration and commiseration. One simple change has made a big difference. Each consultation room, as *Management Lessons from Mayo Clinic* author Leonard Berry has observed, features a specially designed, multipurpose couch instead of a couple of chairs, a setup that rarely affords enough seating for everyone who needs to be present.

You may not think the relationship-conduit model applies to every business situation, but it applies quite widely. The True Value Hardware store and the CVS Minute Clinic seem purely functional at first glance, so putting a priority on facilitating customer relationships there appears beside the point. But even mundane, transactional situations common to the Minute Clinic or a hardware store can be improved by keeping an eye out for how relationships among customers can be facilitated. A Minute Clinic is a lot more comfortable for the patient if the patient's family has a place to sit as well; the same goes for a customer at True Value if there are changing tables (for when you bring the family) and aisles wide enough to accommodate a shopping companion who gets around via wheelchair.

Help Your Customers Collect Social Currency

Drybar encourages relationships between its customers in several ways. With permission, Drybar posts before-and-after photos of customer blowouts on Facebook and Instagram, whereupon fans critique and comment on the transformations, in some cases selecting certain winners to "hang" on Drybar's Facebook-based wall of fame.

The Drybar mobile app has sharing functionalities built right into it as well. When a customer makes an appointment, she's invited to share it with friends (who may parlay this originally solo invitation into a real-life Drybar meetup). But offering these social media features would mean little if the company didn't make its physical space conducive to gatherings beyond the solo flyby or two friends catching up. The comfortable, open yet sound-level-aware layout in Drybar makes it a natural choice for birthday parties for nearly all ages as well as for girls' nights out, bachelorette parties, sweet sixteens and more.

Drybar's success in triggering such an energetic level of customer sharing raises a good question. Why do customers decide to share? One reason worth considering is the idea that a customer shares in order to elevate her status. A photo of a superb meal at a top restaurant is a source of pride as much as a memento (such as a souvenir menu) would be. Elevating status isn't necessarily about spending money somewhere fancy; it can be a well-planned excursion to an isolated yurt that's proudly shared socially, for example. Status these days looks different than it did in the old, more marketer-driven age of clearly graduated status increments such as the climb from Chevy to Cadillac.

One way purchases and experiences can increase a customer's status is by turning your customer into a "discoverer" in the eyes of his friends, loved ones and casual acquaintances. As a study by The Futures Company recently showed, customers are taking more and more pride in discovering things for themselves—including products and services for sale—and in being recognized by their peer group for being "first." The medium of exchange, in other words, is social currency. And any effort and creativity you can invest in finding ways to help customers collect this social currency for use in building and maintaining their own relationships with others will simultaneously help your business.

Lattes and Laptops: Accommodating "Alone Together" Time

I wrote this chapter in a booth at a charming, funky diner a couple of blocks from my home. On its face, this makes little sense. I have other places where I can work, yet I choose to work here—and have for years in a variety of diners and similar noisy (but not too noisy) public spaces.

I'm not the only one doing private work in public. Today's customers, millennials in particular, are doing a lot of the same, a phenomenon businesses need to be aware of. The Futures Company has dubbed this the "Latte and Laptop" businessperson: the guest, customer or traveler who craves a communal setting where, paradoxically, she can do private work. As designer David Rockwell puts it, younger customers "want flexible public spaces and open layouts that provide them with different options to work and socialize."

"Millennials don't want what they do to be predetermined by [inflexible] architecture," Rockwell continues. Many kinds of business can accommodate and benefit from this phenomenon by harnessing the power of shared experiences and the way that visible sharing tends to lead to more and more people wanting to share an experience as time goes on. Restaurants, coffee shops, even gyms have been adapting to this behavior, working to make spaces and social groupings more fluid. As has an unlikely pioneer in an unlikely industry. Umpqua Bank, a retail bank with branches throughout the Pacific Northwest as well as in California, has transformed its branches into hip places to do your banking, have some coffee and check your email—this last item dovetailing nicely with the partly online/ partly in-person hybrid account-management options that Umpqua has started to offer. In the process, they've turned banking from a private chore into a quasi-social pleasure. Banking especially intrigues because the social dynamics of the banking experience have traditionally occurred between bank employee and customer. With so much of that going away, the move to a stage-for-relationships model may reach the increasingly maligned commercial banking industry just in time.

7

The Value of Values and Transparency

A consumer trend that flies in the face of economic efficiency is quietly gaining steam in the marketplace, especially (but not only) among millennial customers. When millennials do business with a company, they're more likely than previous generations to care about that company's social values: its social responsibility, sustainability and ethics in treating employees and suppliers, according to research by Boston Consulting Group and Barkley. They will reward your company if its behavior matches their own ethics and punish you if it doesn't. And this phenomenon is spilling outward from the millennial demographic. Regardless of their age, customers today have unprecedented choices available to them, a situation that has created an opportunity to buy based on convictions, which was a much harder task decades ago.

Truthiness and Consequences

A business that wants to win the hearts of today's consumers benefits from standing for something and meaning it. "Meaning it" is key: Customers are always on the lookout for corporate hypocrisy. One test for gauging an organization's trustworthiness is whether it engages in greenwashing, the practice of merely paying lip service to environmental issues. Greenwashing is considered bad enough on its own, but customers also feel it likely indicates hypocrisy at the company concerning other ethical issues. These sins include the more general phenomenon called "causewashing," where companies put up a façade of sympathetic labor practices, community involvement, ethical dealings with vendors, humane treatment of animals and more. One millennial I interviewed told me, "People my age are especially attuned to and adept at figuring out if a company is being pro-people or pro-environment in its marketing, and anti-people or anti-environment in its actions."

With social media ubiquitous and "inside information" a Google search away, an organization can't hope to hide its hypocrisy for long. A causewashing company, or any company that appears to differ between its words and its deeds, can find itself flayed online before it knows what happened. When Lululemon showed reluctance to take responsibility for a see-through yoga-pants debacle, it turned off customers, who had previously considered the company a paragon of New Age virtue, to the tune of a 50% drop in share price (as of this writing). You'd do better as a company to emulate Starbucks and strive for honest marketing practices, walking the talk of your corporate philosophy. The coffee giant spends more than it needs to spend on coffee beans to buy only the most ethically sourced beans. It also shells out (heh) more on employee compensation by insisting on giving health insurance to every part-time worker, not just to the company's full-timers.

A Rundown of Millennial Values

Since millennials in particular buy where their values lie (whenever they can afford to), businesses will benefit from knowing what those values entail:

- They support workers' rights. According to Pew, 78% of millennials agree with the statement, "Labor unions are needed to protect the rights and economic well-being of workers." With or without unions, they strongly support the idea that companies should treat employees well and pay them fairly.
- They believe company values should go beyond corporate self-interest. In general, millennials disagree with the notion that a business's only

responsibilities are to its shareholders and to watching the bottom line, according to studies cited by Van den Bergh and Behrer. Millennials' faith in the free market sank in 2008 with the stock market, housing prices, their parents' retirement funds and their own employment prospects. Far from supporting an "it's all about the bottom line" philosophy of business, their ethos is closer to something like the "triple bottom-line" equation that Southwest Airlines strives to follow: Our Performance, Our People and Our Planet.

- They believe, by and large, that the role of government is to help, agreeing more than older generations with the sentiment "Government should do more to solve problems," according to Pew. In one example of this inclination, polls have shown that 80% of millennials support universal healthcare in the U.S.

- They want to protect the environment. Millennials harbor a deep-seated support for environmentally friendly action. This is something the millennial generation has believed in since childhood and that shows no sign of slowing down, perhaps in part because this is the first generation to grow up with an overwhelming scientific consensus pointing to manmade climate change.

- They're tolerant. Pew surveys consistently demonstrate that this generation is more supportive of minorities on issues of race, more tolerant of interracial dating, more supportive of gay marriage, more in favor of unmarried adults cohabitating, more approving of mothers working who have young children, and more likely by far to have a close gay friend than do members of older generations.

- They support diversity. From Pew again: Almost twice the percentage of millennials agree with the statement that "we should make every possible effort to improve the position of blacks and other minorities, even if it means giving them preferential treatment" than do members of previous generations. On the issue of immigration, only one-third of millennials agree with the statement that "immigrants threaten American values and customs."

Unprecedented in Their Own Diversity

Millennials' support for diversity is no doubt affected by how diverse this generation is itself. Millennials are by far the most varied cohort in U.S. generational history.

If you were looking to generalize Boomers or the Silent Generation in the U.S., a good guess would be "they're all white." You'd be wrong, but not by all that much. Ninety percent of the Silent Generation is white (80% are non-Hispanic white), and even among Boomers, 73% are non-Hispanic white. The makeup of the millennial generation is far different. Only 61% of millennials are non-Hispanic whites (this percentage is similar to that in the smaller Gen X), and millennials are more likely than any generation since the Silent Generation to be the children of immigrants. (All figures here are from Pew research.) Even these numbers don't fully demonstrate the impact of this diversity. Take note that these "minorities" (hardly the right term) are far from evenly dispersed across the country, and are disproportionately represented in cities. In metropolises of significant size around the country, "minority" (Hispanic, Asian-American and black) groups together make up the majority.

This diversity is well represented in purchasing decisions. Among millennials in the all-important business traveler segment, the proportion of Hispanics is 60% higher, the percentage of Asian-Americans double and the percentage of women is 40% higher than it is among non-millennial business fliers, according to Boston Consulting Group.

Transparency Is Key

Transparency is a corporate attribute that millennials particularly value. And transparency is a quality no business can superficially slap atop its brand.

"I look for total transparency in a company I buy from—or, for that matter, work for," says Adriana Dunn, a customer behavior expert at StellaService and a millennial herself. "I want to know what's behind the brand." Two brands that Dunn singled out for making transparency a cornerstone of their business practices are Everlane and Honest by. Everlane offers designer goods with transparent pricing and sourcing: Vendor practices, markup, and materials and production processes are laid out online for all to see. Honest by sells luxury brands with complete sourcing transparency. Its openness corresponds to its lengthy ethical statement, part of which follows:

> We conduct extensive research into the sources of the raw materials, we trace back the origins of fabrics and trimmings used in the products to be certain that every element in each garment is as environmentally friendly as possible, that the well-being of the client's skin is taken into consideration and that the working conditions in the production facilities are safe, for every product we sell. Honest by chooses not to distribute leather goods or clothes that are made or trimmed with fur, shell or horn. The only animal products our selections do contain are wool and silk. The wool used in the garments is either certified organic, recycled or sourced from selected farms in countries like the UK, where laws on farming ensure the welfare of animals …

Transparency in Customer Support

Applegate, a successful purveyor of humanely raised and slaughtered meats, employs a transparent self-service approach to customer service, making use of a community software platform called "Get Satisfaction." Applegate regularly fields specific, detailed and emotionally charged questions about both its meat and the packaging in which it is conveyed. Rather than solely rely on its employees to answer these questions, Applegate openly crowd-sources commentary and advice from other customers to answer these questions honestly. By using the feedback from customers who have already explored these kinds of questions, Applegate is making transparency work in its favor, elevating the customer and its products at the same time.

JD Peterson, the former VP of marketing for Zendesk, a prominent customer support SaaS platform, points out that the millennial need for recognition and feedback drives the push toward crowdsourcing: "Let your power users be the voice [of your brand]. Customers these days are more willing to do this kind of work for your brand, but they want recognition for doing it—they would like to be given that badge or stamp that says, 'You're the power expert in Applegate bacon.' Giving power users that recognition, a badge, points [or] some sort of title, giving them something they can stamp on their resume or their LinkedIn profile that says they're an expert or a power user, I think, is really important to customers today. It's certainly a win for [the] business as well. You're not having to take on all the burden of support costs because your users are able to do some of that for you—and your customers get closer to the brand at the same time by assisting you."

Ratings and review transparency is likewise an important commercial trend: from voluntary transparency on sites like amazon.com that openly show customer ratings for all products (including sometimes mixed reviews for Amazon's own Kindle tablets and Fire phone), to enforced transparency via TripAdvisor, Yelp and the like that post reviews of your services and products whether you want to be rated this way or not. Embrace this trend even when it's uncomfortable, because it's not going away. Reviews are now decentralized and user driven, and you can't control product ratings, product discussions or much else in the way of reviews, except by providing the best customer experience possible and by being proactive in responding to negative trends that come to the surface in your reviews and ratings.

Emulate a company like Engine Yard, a San Francisco-based cloud application management platform that has taken the brave step of putting a real-time (not to mention cute and cuddly) indicator of its current customer satisfaction stats right on its support site. You'll find 100 panda icons featured prominently on Engine Yard's website with just a few "sad pandas" crossed out in red. Looking at the company's site as of this writing I see 97 happy pandas and three that are crossed out, indicating a current 97% customer satisfaction rating. How does Engine Yard arrive at the proportion of happy and sad pandas? Each time there's a support interaction, Engine Yard asks the customer, "Are you satisfied with the response you got? Yes or no?" It then totals that percentage on its website for anyone to see.

TripAdvisor, Yelp and other user-empowering sites have made customers the most powerful they've ever been. Now every customer has, or feels she has, a "vote" in how companies do business and treat customers. This is part of a new set of expectations among customers today that will only grow stronger. Customers expect to be acknowledged. Those businesses most successful at communicating with today's customers are scrupulous about acknowledging feedback and replying to those providing feedback, whether in person or online. Customers expect companies to change to suit them. Because of the perceived power of their online voices, they now believe companies should change the way they do business to meet their expectations. Customers also want access to the people at the top. Whether it is a CEO or the president of the United States, social media users feel they should have access to those in power. It's worth acknowledging, and embracing, these expectations.

8

Redefine Loyalty (A Bit)

I've been hearing nervous chatter in the business press lately about the supposed waning of customer loyalty. Customers, so this story goes, have become more prone to switching between companies and brands than they've ever been before.

But what's the real story? Can modern-day customers become and remain faithful to a company, a brand or a superior customer experience? In my research and experience, I've repeatedly seen that the answer is yes, but getting there requires a caveat or two plus a few adjustments in thinking.

The 10% Solution

It's undoubtedly true that customers have more purchasing options than ever before, as well as fewer obstacles if they want to switch to a different supplier. This embarrassment of riches strains traditional notions of loyalty. But it hardly spells the end for retention, not for customers in general and certainly not for millennials, despite what many claim. In actuality, Boston Consulting Group research has shown that younger millennials (ages 18 to 24 at the time of the study), "are three times more likely to report strong brand loyalty than their non-millennial counterparts."

If my take on this sounds more hopeful than what you've heard elsewhere, it's partly because my definition of customer loyalty differs from most.

In everything I do, I aim for what I call "90% loyal" customers—the ones who will stick with you through thick or thin, good times or bad, *most* of the time.

This 10% wiggle room makes the loyalty goal a bit more achievable by bringing the concept of loyalty more in line with what's realistic.

Most of My Loving

Every one of us in business knows the score: If a sexy new restaurant or shop opens across the street from ours, even our best customers are going to want to try it—once. But they'll be back once their itch for novelty, their fleeting need to cheat on their main squeeze, has passed.

And sometimes, it's not this need for novelty that makes customers stray from you periodically. Practicality may demand it. A 90%-loyal Whole Foods dad may do some shopping at Trader Joe's or Wegmans when he's stuck in a different part of town. And if Mom's preferred airline doesn't have a direct flight while another carrier does, this otherwise loyal passenger will most likely take the direct flight if that's what it takes to get home in time for her kid's soccer game.

Even the ever-competitive Richard Branson once recommended that his customers use archrival British Airways—if only to remind themselves why they love Branson's Virgin Airlines all the more. Of course, Branson being Branson, he timed his recommendation for the day British Airways offered a fire sale that he knew Virgin couldn't affordably counter, and on which British Airways was sure to lose money.

Building a Home for Your Customers

To ensure your customers are motivated to return to you after they've satisfied their wanderlust and curiosity elsewhere, you need to create a "home" for them, an experience that forges a real relationship with your one-time buyers and gives them an inclination to return.

In other words, if you want to turn your one-time customers into regulars, strive to create an environment, product, process and/or service that feels, in a sense, like home to them. Naturally, customers don't want a business to resemble their homes literally, in the sense of dirty dishes in the sink, gunked-up gutters and so on. What customers want from a business resembles the home environment they remember from (or imagine of) childhood. In a customer's childhood home, she ideally enjoyed a different sort of experience from what life as an adult has become. Food in the fridge was stocked to suit her personal preferences. Light bulbs were changed before she even noticed them flickering. When she left to go to school, her parents would say goodbye in a way that made it clear she would be missed, and they would welcome her back warmly when she returned.

So how does this apply to your ability to foster the desire of your customers to return? Much of it boils down to recognition: Acknowledge your customers, let them know you *see* them, that you respect and anticipate their preferences, that you've missed them in their absence and that you appreciate them upon their return. Recognition, to quote restaurateur and master of hospitality Danny Meyer, is "the number one reason guests cite for wanting to return."

This approach builds an environment your customers are likely to return to time and again, a place where they're known, appreciated and feel welcome, and where things suit their preferences. Not only can they get what they want here, the business also knows what they want before they ask for it.

Micro-Loyalty and Portfolio Loyalty

A couple of trends are complicating the loyalty landscape. Customers today are what I'd call micro-loyal: loyal to Apple for this but Google for that, to Reebok for this but Nike for that, and so forth. They don't buy an overall identity related to a single brand; they mix and match. They still consider themselves loyal, but it's a more targeted type of loyalty.

How did this come about? Younger customers today were raised with a lot of support for individuation. They were allowed to make their own choices and work with the results. From mismatched socks (ultimately commercialized by Little Miss Match) to tattoos and piercings to control over hairstyles and how they dress for school, this generation was empowered by its parents to shape its own identity. As marketers and generational researchers Van den Bergh and Behre point out, the Internet has further fostered such mix-and-match identities, at least in the commercial sphere of their lives. Easy-to-find product review sites like Gizmodo make it far easier to sample and choose brands, comparison shopping on mobile phones has long been a reality, and thanks to iTunes and many other sites, even the playlists they listen to are easily stitched together song by song from their own choices rather than by some label's tastemakers.

A related phenomenon—portfolio loyalty—occurs when customers are equally loyal to *every* brand in a small portfolio of trusted brands in a particular category. This behavior wouldn't be possible without the surfeit of choices consumers now have in almost every consumer category. Consumers have the globalization of commerce, improvements in many companies' return policies due to competitive pressure and the various defect-reduction campaigns in manufacturing of the past several decades to thank for all these offerings. (Formerly an automotive punch line, Ford is an impressively reliable manufacturer today. Even a Jaguar—should you be so lucky to drive one—will rarely leave you stranded these days.)

Aggregator Sites Make Loyalty More Complicated

It's no surprise that retail aggregators are increasingly shaping how people buy. Think of Amazon, pretty much unmatched in customer retention thanks to its ease of use, dizzying selection, recommendation engine and friction-free return policies. Or look to Chinese e-commerce titan Alibaba and its historic $21.8 billion IPO this past September. Markets are bullish on the future of retail aggregation, particularly as it happens online, and so are customers. The Boston Consulting Group finding

I quoted earlier—that younger millennials are three times more likely to report strong brand loyalty than are non-millennials—only reflects millennial *preferences*, not necessarily their actions. Like countless others, millennials purchase from aggregators, one factor that's complicating traditional loyalty to brands.

No company specializing in a single line of products can match the breadth of offerings that a company like Amazon offers. And this carries some unnerving implications for business competition. When a fan of Tumi luggage begins a search at Amazon as opposed to Tumi's own website, the results may not break Tumi's way. Amazon's site might point out to the prospective shopper that "people who looked for this item also looked for Briggs & Riley luggage." Suddenly the Tumi bag the shopper originally pined for (hard shell with an extra outer pocket) seems a bit overpriced or slightly off-color. One click over to a Briggs & Riley suitcase is easy to make. The momentum has swung from buying Tumi to purchasing Briggs & Riley; it requires fewer clicks now to complete the Briggs & Riley purchase than to return to the Tumi bag, the original object of the customer's search.

Unfortunately, there's no perfect solution to the platform problem that arises with the Amazons of the world. A site like amazon.com enjoys unmatched efficiencies of scale and peerless fulfillment and logistics expertise. Let's face it: No matter how astounding your brand's own Web presence is, you won't always manage to get a customer to purchase from you directly, thanks to Amazon's advantages with the customer experience it provides. For starters, the customer's credit card is already securely stored with Amazon, which makes ordering from Amazon both convenient and relatively safe, two factors that go a long way in the still-wild west of e-commerce. Then there are Amazon's customer-friendly return policies and procedures, so seamless that they often result in a refund to the customer's account within 30 minutes of the UPS pickup. Furthermore, there's no way to beat Amazon at the low-price game (even though you'd think you should be able to as the source provider) in the long term. Chalk this up to Amazon's willingness to loss-lead to maintain sales and scale, and to customers and bots reporting lower prices back to Amazon constantly, which allows the company to reduce its prices immediately to match or beat whatever other vendors (that would be you) offer. All of which extends Amazon's advantage beyond its unparalleled product variety, the variety that makes it such a mixed bag (even though it's such a necessity for many small companies) to sell on Amazon's site in the first place.

Aggregators aren't going to go away, but there are ways to nudge potential customers toward starting and ending at your own site. Add as much character to your site as possible—aim to make it more of an experience and adventure to buy from you. (See Rockler or Big Ass Fans for two inspiring examples.) But don't offer an experience at the expense of ease, or you'll scare your customers right back to Amazon. The adventure a customer has on your site needs to be a frictionless one: Do whatever it takes to ensure that your checkout process is easy and seamless. Incorporate a Visa Pay or even (yes) an Amazon Payments button into your site if you can. This may seem off-brand but it's a comfort to your customers, since many of them have all their card information at those sites to begin with. Also, your returns process needs to be as simple, fast and personable as the shopping experience itself. Finally, offering free, brand-relevant extras can distinguish a direct purchase. Throwing in something special and surprising for your customers, whether you do it in the actual product shipment or shortly after, helps create a little magic and offers a personal touch that an aggregator shipment lacks.

Another way to distinguish yourself from aggregators involves making your packaging and messaging distinctive. When a customer orders clothing or gear directly from Moosejaw, an outdoor-recreation/apparel retailer, it arrives in a repurposed package (a previously used UPS overnight sack turned inside-out) that says, "NO KNIFE, USE TEETH!" Brooks Brothers distinguishes its shipments with beautiful boxes screened on the inside with the company's insignia, with woven blue-on-white Brooks Brothers ribbon tying up each purchase. The messaging by mail or email that accompanies a shipment can also distinguish your company. HEX, a company that makes "fashion tech accessories," in other words spiffy-looking iPad covers and the like, is a young operation with no marketing budget that competes against established brands like Michael Kors. HEX has grown its business by sending 13,000 handwritten thank-you notes (so far) to its customers. This may sound extremely old-fashioned, difficult to scale and hard to spread via social media (since the thank yous are actual paper notes) but HEX has found that its gestures of thanks find their way online. Many of the brand's fans snap photos of the cards they receive from HEX and share them on Instagram and Twitter. With such efforts, you'll ideally start or continue a dialogue with your customer, rather than ceding that relationship to outside forces. A wok company that sells both directly and through aggregators is a great exemplar of this behavior. Along with each wok shipment, the company includes in its packaging a bamboo backscratcher. This might sound like more of a headscratcher than a backscratcher, until you look more closely: The company (The Wok Shop) has decorated the backscratcher with the word REACHABLE, along with the company's contact information.

Don't Show Customers a Rerun: Keeping the Customer Service Experience Fresh

Humans (including customers) will adapt to any situation, good or bad, over time: What's bad will eventually seem less bad, which is handy, but the good will eventually seem less good as well, which can pose a problem. This is called the principle of hedonic adaptation.

The implication for maintaining customer interest and engagement is this. Once you've initially succeeded in interesting your customers in your brand, once you've succeeded in pleasing them with your customer experience and customer service, you need to work on keeping their interest by adding clues and cues to the plot.

Any initially meaningful element of your customer experience can start to grow stale over time. Service signatures, scripted interactions and product offerings that delighted customers at first will get copied, replicated and bastardized over time. They'll inevitably lose their intended meaning. (Ritz-Carlton Hotel Company's signature phrase, "My pleasure," for instance, has lost some of its freshness now that you can even get a $2.99 rendition of it from a server at Chik Fil A. This has led Ritz-Carlton to change up its language of late to keep it fresh and authentic.)

And, of course, what's fabulous to a customer on visit one will be "fine but nothing new" on visit five. This is a particularly thorny problem in our era of intensive and friction-free social sharing. You need to be providing something fresh to tantalize your customers and encourage them to share.

For a business to stay relevant, it must frequently reinvent itself, including reworking or replacing practices that were once cutting-edge. A friend of mine described to me his reaction to Nordstrom's practice of coming from behind the counter to hand customers their shopping bags. "This was pretty cool the first five times or so. Around the sixth time, it became annoying; it just seemed like they were slowing me down for the sake of their internal ceremony." And I've seen a similar loss of love for the once-fresh idea of printing a guest's name on a menu at a destination restaurant. The first time you see this by your plate, you're undoubtedly impressed. The third or fourth time, you're bored and ready for a new trick.

Businesses need to realize that there's a shelf life for these choreographed service practices and that they'll need to be revised when they start to wear on customers. Remember that your customers are dynamic, creative people; your business should reflect this. To keep today's customers coming back, a business should constantly improve, update and expand its line of products or services where appropriate—which, today, means on a schedule faster than ever before.

On the other hand, change for change's sake is hazardous, because the goal of customer service and the customer experience isn't buzz— it's loyalty. Repeat business is what keeps you alive. While it's true that customers seek innovation from the companies they frequent, if a company *only* invests in change, then how can a customer remain loyal? What is left for them to be loyal to? There's an inherent tension between innovation and tradition, and it's hard to get the mix right. When I interviewed celebrated restaurateur and innkeeper Patrick O'Connell, proprietor of the Inn At Little Washington and president of Relais and Chateaux, he articulated this well: "Cultivating loyalty is a tricky business. It requires maintaining a rigorous level of consistency while constantly adding newness and a little surprise—freshening the guest experience without changing its core identity."

Lifetime Network Value

Concerns about brand fickleness in the new generation of customers can be troubling partly because the idea of lifetime customer value has been such a cornerstone of business for so long. But while you're fretting over the occasional straying of a customer due to how easy it is to switch brands today, don't overlook a more important positive change in today's landscape: the extent to which social media and Internet reviews have amplified the reach of customers' word-of-mouth. Never before have customers enjoyed such powerful platforms to share and broadcast their opinions of products and services. This is true today of every generation—even some Silent Generation customers share on Facebook and post reviews on TripAdvisor and Amazon. But millennials, thanks to their lifetime of technology use and their growing buying power, perhaps make the best, most active spokespeople a company can have.

Boston Consulting Group, with grand understatement, says that "the vast majority" of millennials report socially sharing and promoting their brand preferences. Millennials are talking about your business when they're considering making a purchase, awaiting assistance, trying something on, paying for it and when they get home. If, for example, you own a restaurant, the value of a single guest today goes further than the amount of the check. The added value comes from a process that Chef O'Connell calls competitive dining, the phenomenon of guests "comparing and rating dishes, photographing everything they eat, and tweeting and emailing the details of all their dining adventures."

It's easy to underestimate the commercial power that today's younger customers have, particularly when the network value of these buyers doesn't immediately translate into sales. Be careful not to sell their potential short and let that assumption drive you headlong into a self-fulfilling prophecy. Remember that younger customers are experimenting right now as they begin to form preferences they may keep for a lifetime. And whether their proverbial Winstons will taste good to them in the future depends on what they taste like presently. A little love lavished on these customers now will likely be repaid in spades in the future.

Farewell for Now, and Happy Customering

Learning about the fascinating humans whom we call customers never ends, but this book must. Let me leave you with one thought. Try to keep in mind that every customer, of any age and any industry, is unique. It's *that* customer, the one you're with at the moment of service—face to face, phone to phone, or terminal to terminal—who matters, not some hypothetical you read about in a book, even this one. You can always reach me directly to apply these insights more specifically to your situation at micah@micahsolomon.com or (484) 343-5881. (And I answer my own phone.) Thank you for your time, and happy customering!

Notes

1. *Millennial Passions: Food, Fashion, and Friends* (Boston Consulting Group, 2010)

2. *Traveling With Millennials* (Boston Consulting Group, 2013)

3. *American Millennials: Deciphering the Enigma Generation* (Barkley in collaboration with Service Management Group And Boston Consulting Group, 2011)

4. *Millennial Passions*

5. *Millennial Momentum* (Morley Winograd and Mr. Michael D. Hais, 2011)

6. *IBID*

7. *Millennial Passions*

8. Thank you to Leslie Hand, Vice President, IDC Retail Insights, for this example.

9. *Millennial Passions*

10. *Management Lessons From Cleveland Clinic*, Leonard L. Berry, 2008

11. For details on Google's survey methodology and the source of these scores, please see my Forbes.com article: http://www.forbes.com/sites/micahsolomon/2014/05/05/google/

12. Thanks to Tim Miller for this phrasing.

13. Thanks to Laura Romanoff of the Maya Romanoff Company (my cooler than cool cousin) for talking me through this.

14. *IBID*

Publisher's note: If you are interested in any of the services provided by Micah Solomon, he has invited readers to call 484-343-5881 or to email micah@micahsolomon.com for information.

Services offered:
- Consulting and company initiatives on customer service, the customer experience, and company culture
- Keynote speeches for events of all sizes, anywhere in the world
- Seminars (extended presentations), onsite, anywhere in the world
- Webinars: speeches and seminars delivered to you remotely
- Content creation: articles, columns, whitepapers for print publication, websites and blogs as well as long-form (book-length and eBook) content creation